Praise for *1*

"Some authors open windows offering readers a quick glimpse of their lives, but Colonel Lisa Carrington Firmin pulls the front door wide open, welcoming the reader in with no time by which one must leave, and no topic left unexplored. She takes the reader on a journey with an honor, respect, and safety that was not always afforded her and, in the process, creates an intimacy and trust that keeps the reader engaged, anticipating each page turn, and ultimately rewarded with a feast for the eyes, heart, and mind.

"We saw the power of words and writing in the creative engagements we offered as part of our care of wounded, ill and injured servicemembers at Walter Reed National Military Medical Center and it continued to be true as we moved to a virtual platform during the COVID pandemic, offering writing workshops for patients, caregivers, family members, and staff. These classes, like Writing for Well-being, Writing for Love, and Writing for Grief, filled immediately and the participant's feedback was strong and overwhelmingly supportive. Creativity and self-expression continue to demonstrate their ability and role in finding and maintaining health, balance, and well-being.

"The power of using art to express oneself and illustrate lived experiences is strongly evident throughout the poetry and art in *Latina Warrior*. This unique collaboration can serve as a blueprint for others to start and traverse their own healing journeys."

— **Captain Moira G. McGuire**, US Public Health Service (Ret.)
Former Chief, Arts in Health Program, National Intrepid Center of Excellence
Founder, Healing Arts Exhibit, Walter Reed

"Lisa Carrington Firmin's fierce and brutally honest autobiography in verse takes the reader from childhood, to the ravages of combat, to the reconciled reality of life among civilians. This book is not just for veterans, but for anyone seeking to understand the warrior's experience in combat or a smart, driven Latina's experience of life before, during, and after military service. A searing avalanche of images and words that jointly document and illustrate a Latina warrior's life."

— **Norma Elia Cantú**, author of *Canícula: Snapshots of a Girlhood en la Frontera*, Murchison Professor of Humanities at Trinity University, San Antonio, Texas

"*Latina Warrior* challenges the public mindset of military service, as these strong and courageous women combat veterans share their most intimate experiences, revealing the obstacles, realities, and success of their military service and found sisterhood. This collaboration between Colonel Carrington Firmin and Major Helferich-Polosky epitomizes selfless leadership, as the richly illustrated poems open channels for readers to gain insight into the challenges that women and minorities face both in the military and after. A rare glimpse into the realities of military women's service and a demonstration of the uplifting power of military sisterhood."

— **AnnMarie Halterman**, USAF veteran and artist
  Co-founder, Uniting US

"These poems are raw and real, coming from the perspective of a Latina warrior. Fellow combat veteran Helferich-Polosky's accompanying artwork adds an important visual dimension. The poems capture stories that need to be told so others know they are not alone, especially those who have experienced military sexual trauma. They reflect Carrington Firmin's life journey from growing up as a Latina, to joining the military and experiencing combat, to life after the military and a shifting identity that so many service members experience, and, ultimately, to healing as an "MST Warrior." She finds the courage to speak her truth through her poems, along the way finding her strength and a place of healing that is inspirational to others."

— **Sandra B. Morissette, PhD**
  Professor of Psychology, The University of Texas at San Antonio

50 POEMS
by a
Latina Warrior

LISA CARRINGTON FIRMIN

Original art by Christina Helferich-Polosky

BLUE EAR BOOKS

Published in 2023 by
Blue Ear Books
7511 Greenwood Ave N, Box 400
Seattle, WA 98103
USA

www.blueearbooks.com

Copyright © Lisa Carrington Firmin

The right of Lisa Carrington Firmin to be identified as the author of the work has been asserted by her in accordance with the Copyright, Designs, and Patents Act of 1988.

All rights reserved. No part of this publication may be reproduced, stored in a retrieval system, or transmitted in any form or by any means, electronic, mechanical, photocopying, recording, or otherwise, without prior written permission of the author or the publisher.

ISBN: 978-0-9990951-2-6

Cover design: Sean Robertson
Author back cover photograph by Matt Roberts
Photos in art pieces 12, 32, 33, 40, 42, 44, 46: Natalie Dohman, nDesign Art Haus, LLC
Page design: Jennifer Haywood, Blue Ear Books

For my veteran sisterhood, Latinas, and women everywhere: dream way bigger than you think is possible, let nothing hold you back, for anything can be achieved with ganas.

For my mom and dad, whose endless love and life lessons took firm root and laid the foundation for the warrior I would become.

For my son, whose many sacrifices growing up with a mother in combat boots can never be repaid: know that I will spend the rest of my life trying. Te amo mucho mi querido hijo.

    - Lisa Carrington Firmin

To all my sisters in arms, who strive to struggle well each day: please make the time to create one thing for yourself today and support each other always. I salute you.

To Mom and Dad, I finally see why you gave me roots and wings all those years ago: so I can fly my way home.

To Jacob: first out of the gate, my apologies. Thank you for teaching me what forgiveness looks like. You're gorgeous.

To Michael: it hasn't been easy, middle son, finding your way. Thank you for teaching me control; you're a natural.

To Anthony: youngest son, my brilliant friend, the one that always gets caught. Thank you for teaching me how to laugh at myself. Don't worry, it gets better.

And to Hannah, the baby Willow branch of this bunch, within whom so much talent, passion and promise already resides: roots and wings my love, roots and wings.

    - Christina Helferich-Polosky

Trigger Warning

This book includes poems, prose, and art that might be triggering for some due to their content involving sexual assault, discrimination, and combat.

PTSD/MST resources:

VA:
https://www.mentalhealth.va.gov/msthome/
https://www.mentalhealth.va.gov/ptsd/

DoD Sexual Assault Prevention and Response Office:
https://www.sapr.mil/

RAINN (Rape, Abuse & Incest National Network):
https://www.rainn.org/

CONTENTS

Introduction 1

Early Years y Familia

1. Globetrotter 7
2. Big Bro 9
3. Flaca 11
4. La Manguera 13
5. First Gen 15
6. In the Bleachers 17
7. Tomasita 19
8. Valley Girl 21
9. Javelinas 23
10. Home 25
11. The Boy, The Man, and The Father 27
12. Mis Amigas 29
13. Bear 31
14. Ay Mijita 33

The Military and Combat

15. Taps 37
16. Snowflakes from Above 39

17. Ode to a White Dude...........................41
18. Every Day Was Tuesday 43
19. DALT..45
20. Christian in a Foxhole........................47
21. The Combat You...............................49
22. Eye Fuckery...................................51
23. Black Death...................................53
24. Echoes of War................................55
25. Cocktail......................................57
26. Command.....................................59
27. Guerrera Latina 61
    Latina Warrior 63

Life after the Military

28. Transition Blisters 67
29. Invisible Veteran..............................69
30. Superwoman Is Dead..........................71
31. Save the Civilians.............................73
32. The Sisterhood................................75
33. You Get Me...................................77
34. Get Out of My Head 79
35. VetSpeak.....................................81
36. Death of a Wife...............................83
37. Death of a Marriage..........................85

38. Not an Imposter 87

39. Mi Pastora 89

Healing and the Road to Authenticity

40. Into the Light 93

41. MST Warrior 97

42. The Grunt and the Colonel 99

43. La Rona/The Trickster 101

44. Fractured 103

45. The Abyss 105

46. The Breakup 107

47. Pain 109

48. Wounded Not Worthless 111

49. Life 113

50. Writing Is My Salvation 115

Reflections from the Poet and Artist 117

Afterword by Dr. Pat Pernicano 169

Acknowledgements 173

About the Author 181

About the Artist 182

Introduction

The book you hold in your hands is my rebirth, my entry into finally living an authentic life. To write it, I had to do the painful deep reflection that usually accompanies such a voyage. I started writing poetry in 2021, following an extremely reflective period throughout 2020 while I was isolated due to Covid, living with increased pain from service-connected disabilities, and reeling from the horrific murder of soldier Vanessa Guillén. I found that those first poems helped me deal better with my pain, my past trauma, and life's challenges. Words became my release, a way to use artistic expression to help me move beyond pain and start to heal deeply buried wounds. My journey spans decades and begins in the hot, humid South Texas valley of my people, winds its way across the United States and to other countries, detours for a combat stint in Iraq's Sunni Triangle, then continues back in the USA with many starts, stops, and off ramps.

Latina Warrior is not your typical book of poems and art. It is a hybrid work of collaborative autobiography by two highly decorated women combat veterans. Although it is my story, the poems, prose, and art are the stories of both of us, and they just might provide a revealing glimpse into your story as well. I first met my fellow Bronze Star-decorated combat veteran Christina Helferich-Polosky in 2021 at the Military Women's Memorial at Arlington National Cemetery, where we both had items on display. We met again the following year at the Library of Congress, as part of a group of veteran artists that Uniting US had pulled together to share our work specifically regarding PTSD and military sexual trauma (MST), both of which unfortunately are in my wheelhouse. It was my first genuine experience of publicly sharing, specifically aimed at healing through the arts.

I really got to know Christina when I interviewed her, along with her mother and grandmother, for an article I was writing about generations of service within one family. I knew then that I wanted to collaborate with her on the *Latina Warrior* journey. I was super stoked when she agreed to illustrate each poem with original art. I love her art. It is telling and so remarkably diverse, exactly what I dreamed could accompany my poems. I find myself having to look at her pieces multiple times, since I know a cursory look would miss something. I am so grateful that Christina stepped up to the challenge when my initial vision of twenty to thirty poems became fifty poems. The collaboration has been healing for both of us, and the back-and-forth discussion on how to depict certain pieces was empowering.

Never quite believing I was a poet, I was amazed that my first two poems, "Into the Light" and "Save the Civilians," were put on display at the Military Women's Memorial and Dulles International Airport. The first deals with me speaking up, after many years of silence, about having been sexually assaulted in initial training in the military. The second tells the story of a PTSD flashback episode I experienced. The reaction to both was overwhelming. So many individuals related to me that the poems spoke to and validated their own experiences. I realized that I was onto something: not only could I help myself in healing, but perhaps the simple act of sharing my own story could help others.

My early poems were all written from pain, anger, and trauma-filled memories. I worried that I might not be able to write about the joys in my life, but I discovered that those first poems became a way for me to wrestle with the pain, to never forget but to learn to live with it, so that I could progress further. This worry was short-lived, as I have indeed been able to write about joy and happiness and am basking in that self-discovery.

I honor my Latina culture and pay homage to my often-perilous journey in the military and struggles to fit in, my transition back into civilian life, and my leadership trials. I also share my very personal journey of healing from trauma. I divided *Latina Warrior* into four parts: Early Years y Familia, Military and Combat, Life after the Military, and Healing and the Road to Authenticity.

These poems run the gamut from South Texas "Valley Girl" to a despicable experience with "Eye Fuckery," to the devastating effects of "Black Death" from burn pits in the combat environment. "Taps" describes the absolute trepidation I felt as my perpetrator's footsteps echoed in the barracks hallway. "Not an Imposter" details my battle with imposter syndrome. "The Combat You" speaks intensely about how, post-combat, I am a totally different person. "Mi Pastora" is a tribute to my amazing Latina pastor. In "Tomasita," "In the Bleachers," and "Big Bro" I honor my family.

A word about the language. I use Spanglish throughout; I kept it real. This is me, the real me, no longer hiding behind a façade of assimilation or trying to fit *the man's* definition of who I am supposed to be. I am the narrator of my own journey, no longer allowing others to tell my story for me. In my own words, I now own my past, present, and future.

My writing continues to evolve, and I find that I cannot stop writing. It is as if I have unleashed the author and poet in me and now I see the world through those eyes. I see every moment, every experience as a potential poem, story, or book. The pen is, indeed, mightier than the sword. The words I have written and published will be forever shared with the world and just might have the power to change lives, as they have changed my own life. I have traded in my combat armor for my pen, and it has become my superpower unleashed. *Latina Warrior* is my story.

Lisa Carrington Firmin
San Antonio, Texas
November 2023

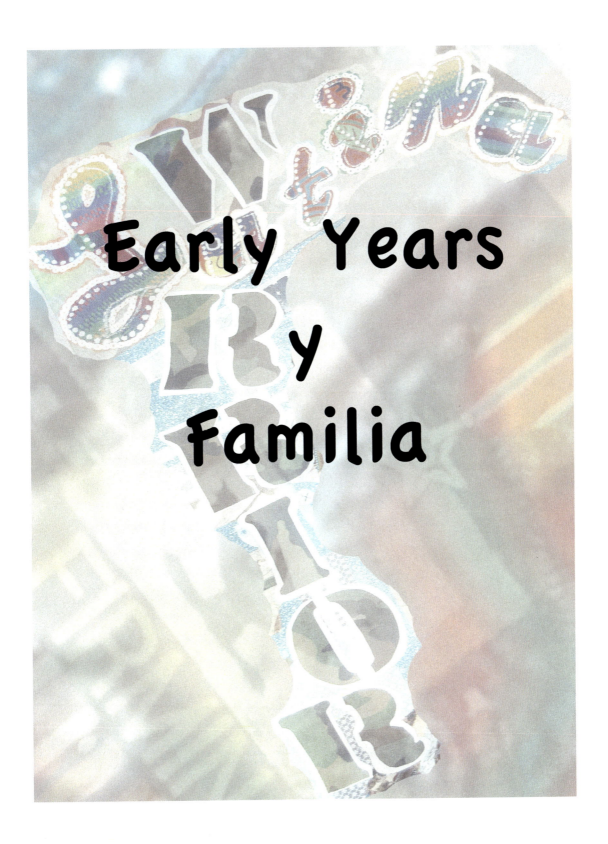

Early Years y Familia

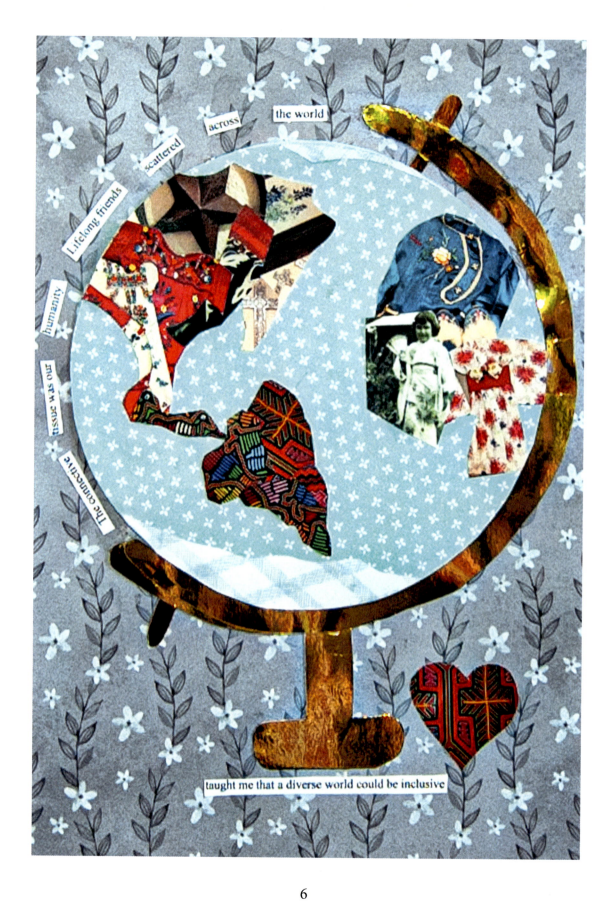

1. Globetrotter

The cream almost white color of the obi belt
cinched the waist of the kimono and
contrasted starkly with the brown of my skin.

Bright intriguing swaths of color
shaped in land, sea, and living designs
adroitly adorned the mola shirt I wore.

The vibrant embroidered dress
along with the cowboy boots on my feet
stood out uniquely to any onlookers.

How extraordinary to experience
my youth among different peoples and nations.
To be accepted freely without hesitation.

Each culture was valued, honored, and respected.
Growing up I knew where I was by the clothes,
and the food, language, and culture all around me.

The connective tissue was our humanity.
Lifelong friends scattered across the world
taught me that a diverse world could be inclusive.

Privileged beyond belief to grow up as a globetrotter,
to live, learn, and love among other cultures, to not fear,
as our similarities were much stronger than our differences.

Big Bro
By Colonel Lisa Carrington Firmin, USAF Ret

Thanks for cutting the hair off my dolls
    Tearing the eyes off my teddy bears
    Disfiguring my barbies
    For teaching me that material things didn't matter

Thanks for posing with me for all those family Easter pics
    Tossing the ball around, playing hoops and coaching me on sports
    Changing clothes before school because I had the exact same overalls on
    For being my only friend when we showed up at a new base

Thanks for making me ask *la senora en la tienda* how much the candy cost
    Being my first competitor; in our parent's attention, sports, academics *y mas*
    Teaching me how to fight and that shiner you gave me once
    For toughening me up and making sure I knew how to defend myself

Thanks for all the tough, hard-won life lessons
    Being my confidant big bro; then, now, and forever
    The privilege and honor to officiate at your military retirement
    For outranking me as an SES

Thanks for loving me even when you hated me
Hermano mio, te quiero mucho.

2. Big Bro

Thanks for cutting the hair off my dolls
      Tearing the eyes off my teddy bears
      Disfiguring my barbies
      For teaching me that material things didn't matter

Thanks for posing with me for all those family holiday pics
      Tossing the ball around, playing hoops and coaching me on sports
      Changing clothes before school because I had the exact same overalls on
      For being my only friend when we showed up at a new base

Thanks for making me always ask how much the candy cost
      Being my first competitor: for our parents' attention, in sports, in academics y mas
      Teaching me how to fight and that shiner you gave me once
      For toughening me up and making sure I knew how to defend myself

Thanks for all the tough, hard-won life lessons
      Being my confidant big bro; then, now, and forever
      The privilege and honor to officiate at your military retirement
      For outranking me as an SES

Thanks for loving me even when you hated me
Hermano mio, te quiero mucho.

3. Flaca

Born average height and weight.
The toddler years brought fat rolls
And lots of dark curly black hair
Quickly morphed into La Gorilita

Mis tios y tias alternated between La Gorilita and Menudo
These weren't great nicknames, but what could I say?
Barely talked, just a little kid that lurched around like Frankenstein
As I started to walk, fat rolls drew more attention to my Menudo

Childhood years turned into adolescence
Bringing all arms and legs, gangly and ill fitting
Took some time for me to grow out of the green bean stage
Picked up yet another nickname: Flaca

Was constantly teased about being skinny and a tomboy
Started wearing glasses, so folks called me Four Eyes
Seems I was always being called names other than my own
Except when I was in trouble, then it was both first and middle names

And I did get into trouble more often than some
So I put my energies into all kinds of sports
My body had finally caught up with my arms and legs
Became a decent athlete in multiple sports

Flaca still comes up among familia when we are together
It's part of me; the nickname carries the weight of endearment
La Gorilita lasted the toddler stage, super happy it and Menudo didn't stick
Admittedly, about now I could use more dark curly hair y less panza.

La Manguera

Always outside
We played hard, laughing all the time
All scraped knees and elbows

Rode our bikes everywhere
Skated and skateboarded
Swung from trees in the jungle

Always outside
Kick ball, softball and basketball
Made up silly pranks and games

No fancy inside water for us
Afuera con la manguera
We greedily drank from that coiled snake

Always outside
La manguera was our friend
The lifeline in the heat

4. La Manguera

Always outside
We played hard, laughing all the time
All scraped knees and elbows

Rode our bikes everywhere
Skated and skateboarded
Swung from trees in the jungle

Always outside
Kickball, softball and basketball
Made up silly pranks and games

No fancy inside water for us
Afuera con la manguera
We greedily drank from that coiled snake

Always outside
La manguera was our friend
The lifeline in the heat

5. First Gen

17 years old, scared and full of a fake confidence,
I showed up at Javelina Nation
believing I could do it, be the first en la familia to finish college

Totally bombed my first semester
But man, it was so much fun
Drank, partied, and stayed out late, away from home at last!

Then reality quickly set in
Couldn't behave this way AND finish college
Something had to change. I dug deep and released my ganas

It became my superpower, turbocharged me to be first gen
Stopped the partying, no more skipping class, hung out in the library
Actually read the lessons, engaged with faculty and staff

All this became the secret sauce to graduating
Despite feeling totally like an outsider
I found community, was no longer alone.

Learned how to tame
the imposter syndrome and crushing weight of intimidation
that I felt almost daily.

I earned my place and degree
finishing in three years with honors
wiping out all the naysayers and my own self-doubt

20 years old, feeling invincible, I made it!
Proudly wearing my First Gen badge
No one can ever take that heavyweight title away.

6. In the Bleachers

Rain or shine he was always there.
In the bleachers no matter the weather
Watching and waiting

My biggest fan
Showed up to all my sporting events
But kept his distance

Didn't really show devotion publicly
Not as a fan in the bleachers
But he sure as heck poured it on at home.

My biggest fan was my dad
Cheered me on, even when I fell short on the field or in the pool
Coached me on how to achieve excellence graciously

I make that last stroke in the water and hit the wall
Then look up in the bleachers to see my biggest fan with a grin
that is both wide and proud. I must have medaled.

Thanks, Dad, for pushing me to do more, to be stronger,
for encouraging me through both victory and defeat,
and showing me that with ganas anything is possible in sports and in life.

7. Tomasita

Saw my reflection in the car window
Wasn't me looking back
It was Tomasita.

Mom, is that you?
Oh, how I long to hear your voice,
to see you and get un abrazo

I miss you so!
Your legacy lives on in all those you touched
None more so than those of us with your blood

Your godly wisdom, spiritual leadership, and selfless acts
remain with us as we try to emulate your actions
I try but never quite make it.

Words cannot do you justice
You were the foundation for la familia
Sacrificed so very much for others

Your love was endless, indeed a sanctuary
Thanks for keeping my sibs and me safe
For teaching us a solid Christian foundation

You didn't have to throw la chancla
Just one look from you kept us in line
We never wanted to let you down.

The matriarch of so many life lessons
As each year passes and I resemble you more
The woman in me prays I can be at least half the woman you were.

8. Valley Girl

I'm a valley girl
No, not that kind
I'm from the 956 baby!

En el sur de Tejas
Affectionately called el valle
30 miles from México

Crossed over when it was safe
Enjoyed cabrito y margaritas
Con mis tios, tias, primos y primas

Each occasion brought la familia together
We broke bread, celebrated life, and shared stories
Laughed, cried, and danced at weddings y mas

Lovingly recall the very special times
when mariachis serenaded Mom and others
with las mananitas to commemorate milestone birthdays

Hung out and chilled in Tamezville
Not quite a real city, but the street of mi gente
Hardworking and proud people, us Tamezes

We picked oranges, grapefruits, lemons and ate our fill
Swam in the dirty canal and imagined we were in a real pool
Teased each other as we munched on chicharron with the hairs still on

These are some of my memories of the 956
I'm a valley girl who's lived throughout the world
But always remember that it's el valle from where I hail

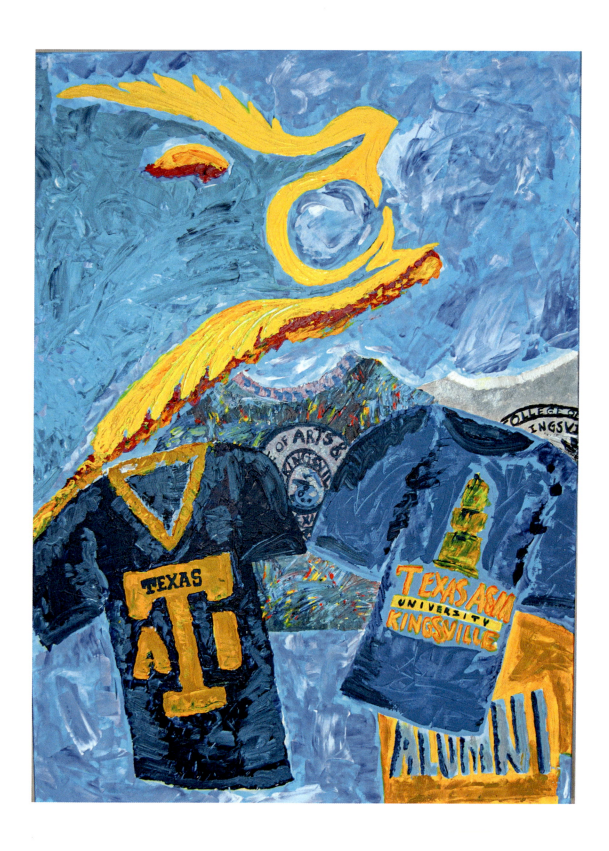

9. Javelinas

I am part of a pack
Never alone, we are much stronger together
Javelinas always have my back

A Javelina is an alum
From Texas A&I or TAMUK
Doesn't matter which, we are all Javelinas

Our traditions and heritage matter
Instant camaraderie when we meet each other
Fierce and proud, we protect and defend the pack

We communicate among ourselves
and network inside and outside our groups
The goal is to lift up all Javelinas, todos adelante

Javelinas strive to be better, to represent
Higher education changed the trajectory of our lives
Strategically positioning us for more opportunity

Hard-fought successes and sacrifices not far from our thoughts
Can never forget where we came from
Javelinas give back, the pack can change the world

We are one institution, una cultura
Doesn't matter when you graduated or if you are A&I or TAMUK
Somos Javelinas.

10. Home

More than 8,000 miles away
Overseas for the first time on my own
Multiple time zones separated me from la familia

I yearn for the taste and smells of home
Nothing shouts mi cultura more than la comida
No better way to feel close to mi gente than to make tamales

The assembly line set up on the dining table
We were like a factory
Everyone had a job to do

You had the spreaders, the fillers and the rollers
All ages involved, listening and learning family history
It was a long and laughter-filled process

Could I really recreate that without la familia?
Never led a tamalada, only a participant
You can do it mijita, Mom says

She sent the family's recipe,
first time she's ever taken the time to write it down
along with hojas de maíz, masa, and spices

I bite into the first tamale
Years of memories flood my senses
The taste and smell a trigger for the good times

Spending time with la familia
en la cocina con mi mamá, tías y primas
the chisme only strengthened the tamale bond

Tasted like home!
Okay, so it took a few tries, had to remake the masa more than once
to get it perfect, so it could take me home in just one bite

11. The Boy, The Man, and The Father

I look at you and see the boy
playing endlessly with swords, ninja turtles, and power rangers
bringing me such unmitigated joy

The boy who played football at three different high schools
in three different states because Uncle Sam dictated where we lived
Am sorry I wasn't there more, hard on us both having a mommy who wore combat boots

I look at you and see the man
finishing college in record time with honors at our alma mater, besting the family record
My heart burst with pride as you walked across the stage in my graduation robe

The man who chose an honorable profession
to ensure law and order and the capacity to provide for a family
Adeptly navigating the struggle for an elusive work-life balance

I look at you and see the father
raising his kids with the Lord guiding your steps
teaching them love, compassion, and the way ahead in a troubled world

The father who sacrifices daily for his children
putting their needs above his, engaging on their level in play, sports, and life
A strong and steady presence

I look at you and see all at once, the boy, the man, and the father
The years fast-forward in my mind, and I am immensely grateful and blessed beyond belief
For you have become the best of what I am, my son, my legacy.

12. Mis Amigas

Strong and powerful women
My own personal board of directors
Rockstars among all my amigos

¡Hermanas fuerte!
Wonder women in so many ways
Fierce at home, at work, and in relationships

When I struggle personally and professionally
A bedrock of unwavering support
Their consejos enrich my life

Anyone throws shade my way
Mis amigas fiercely defend and protect me
Earned the right to fight for me and to call out my shit

Years bring changes across my life
But these hermanas remain steadfast, never judging
No echo chamber here, just real family talk when needed

Mis amigas contribute to my successes
In both small and big ways
As I navigate challenging careers, family, a divorce

Fanatically loyal and honest to the core
Allies, advocates, and amplifiers
Proud to call them Mis Amigas

13. Bear

He was the perfect companion
Looked up at me with those kind brown eyes
Full of compassion and unconditional love

He had a long torso and powerful chest
The ridiculously short legs
barely lifted him off the ground

His long fluffy red-brown hair
kissed the ground with each step he took
Waddled or strutted depending on his mood

He sashayed into my life and won my heart
Couldn't talk but spoke volumes with his remaining eye
Became the one constant when my life was in upheaval

Was there during the passing of my mother,
the pain of a divorce, career evolutions
He soothed me as I grieved and went through transitions

Born when I was in Iraq
Connected in a way I had never experienced before
As if he knew exactly how to comfort me

Bear was more than a best friend
He was family, and I will see him again
one day on the rainbow bridge.

14. Ay Mijita

I rehearsed exactly how I was going to tell my mom
that her daughter was going to war in Iraq
Knew it was not going to be easy

No woman in my family had ever gone to war
Was more afraid of letting my mom know than of actually going
Let's just say it did not go down as I hoped.

What part of me thought I could tell her where I was going?
It was early in the war, most of my troops told their families they
were going to Kuwait or somewhere safe

Few told them it was the Sunni Triangle in Iraq
The location wasn't classified, and I wanted my mom to know
where I would be and how proud I was to go as a commander.

What did she say?
"Ay mijita, can't one of the guys go instead of you?"
I shouldn't have been shocked, but I was

I had worked so hard my entire military career
to overcome barriers, to be an officer, leader and commander.
Had been personally selected to command in Iraq

None of that impressed my mom.
I was her mijita and she feared losing me.
After many tears, lots of talking and filling me with my favorite foods,

she reluctantly acquiesced, contacted our pastor,
started the prayer chain, and set up the baked goods care packages cycle.
I felt her love and prayers every day in the Sunni Triangle.

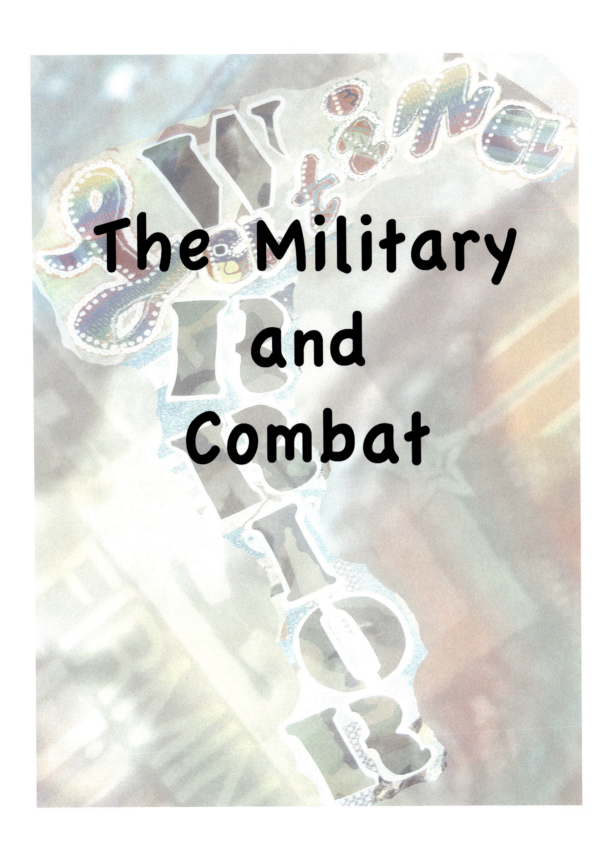

The Military and Combat

15. Taps

I heard him before I saw him
The military taps on his shoes foreshadowed the doom of his arrival
Instantly, I tensed up and feared what was coming.

My jaw clenched, I became like stone
The fear and trepidation were palpable. Was he coming in an official status?
For something training-related?

Or was he coming for some strange obsession he had with me?
I never knew if he would show up as friend or foe
This was my military training instructor.

A man with unfathomable authority over me
Who was sexually harassing me
Then later upped his game to sexual assault

As each of his taps echoed down the hall in the quiet of the barracks
My reaction was Pavlovian
Couldn't control such strong emotions and physical reactions

So, I froze and pretended it wasn't happening to me.
Actually told myself that this might all be just part of the training
To buck up so I could be worthy of becoming a warfighter, a warrior

I dreaded the tap, tap, tap of his shiny black uniform shoes.
The hair on the back of my neck stood up, my heart raced uncontrollably.
The sound of those taps is forever seared in my memory.

16. Snowflakes from Above

Not another one!
I dreaded getting the infamous
Snowflakes from my boss

Meant more work, research or an ass chewing
Rarely was it an "atta girl"
I knew that one "aw shit" wiped out several "atta girls"

Snowflakes fell on my desk as small white memos
from a senior colonel or general officer.
Could be good or bad depending on the message

As an exec, I got plenty. Some were easy to comprehend,
like "PSM" or "SMP":
"Please See Me" or "See Me Please"

Once I got one that simply said "YGTBSM"
A senior colonel was telling me, a junior captain,
"You Got To Be Shitting Me"

Summoned the courage to ask what it all meant.
Told it wasn't about me, but the documents under the memo
Whew, okay so snowflakes could be or not be about me

Wait, that meant that every snowflake
could be about me. Jeez
The pucker factor remained high upon snowflake receipt

17. Ode to a White Dude

Hola white dude, one of a handful
who took a chance years ago
on a young active-duty Latina

Thanks for taking a stand,
stepping up when it wasn't in vogue
to mentor or sponsor "others"

Totally unlike yourself
Someone who was different
in gender and ethnicity

You shared informal rules
of the leadership game
and opened doors and career paths

Thanks for advocating for me
even when I wasn't in the room
and for taking the flak that came with it

You deviated from the norm
demonstrating through action
what real leadership is

It made all the difference in the leader I would become.
Muchismas gracias,
La Coronela

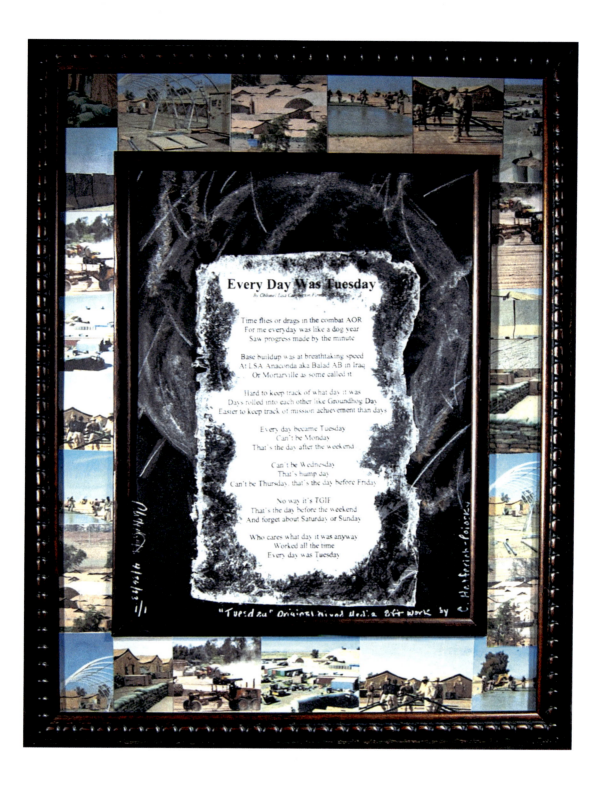

18. Every Day Was Tuesday

Time flies or drags in the combat AOR
For me every day was like a dog year
Saw progress made by the minute

Base buildup was at breathtaking speed
At LSA Anaconda a.k.a. Balad AB in Iraq
Or Mortaritaville as some called it

Hard to keep track of what day it was
Days rolled into each other like Groundhog Day
Easier to keep track of mission achievement than days

Every day became Tuesday
Can't be Monday
That's the day after the weekend

Can't be Wednesday
That's hump day
Can't be Thursday, that's the day before Friday

No way it's TGIF
That's the day before the weekend
And forget about Saturday or Sunday

Who cares what day it was anyway
Worked all the time
Every day was Tuesday

19. DALT

He was a young lieutenant
Very junior, low on the professional ladder
But had grit and moxie enough to share

Stood out immediately, couldn't miss his raw talent
Was more mature than most, his Army experience burst through
Proven performer, especially during mission planning

Leaned on him heavily at AF's inaugural Eagle Flag deployment
Did not disappoint, a proactive and out-of-the-box thinker
Rank didn't hold him back, got things done and spoke his mind

Reminded me of myself at that rank, professional and hungry for more
However, as young Lts often do, he stepped on it more than once
Hence, I gave him a nickname: Dumb Assed Lieutenant

Affectionately shortened to DALT, I took him under my wing
Potential oozed out of him; I began to intentionally mentor
Shared my leadership philosophy along with tough love to level him up

Selected him to serve as my exec in Iraq's Sunni Triangle
He excelled in that combat AOR, was my right and left hand
Our bond forever cemented among rockets and mortars

A mutually satisfying mentorship emerged and survives
Thriving in and out of the military, two-way communication at its core
Proud to officiate at DALT's O-5 military retirement

Will always be DALT to me, but he's so much more
He's my friend, mentee, and colleague, more like a son
Such are the bonds for many that serve.

My body armor and my Lord's armor
always with me
Was a Christian in a Foxhole

20. Christian in a Foxhole

Touched down in the pitch-black dead of night
in Iraq's Sunni Triangle
amid chaff and flares to camouflage our arrival

We scampered rapidly off air transport
similar to journeys of countless warfighters before us
Footfalls quiet and orderly as we marched into a new reality

Burdened by the weight of our gear
The thoughts we carried were heftier, greater than what was on our backs
for we knew the dangers that awaited us

Were lucky to touch down between attacks
Nervous eyes tracking everything about the surroundings
Noting how quickly our pilots departed

They knew it would be minutes before mortars rained down
Welcome to Mortaritaville!
That first attack morphed into hundreds in the days that followed

Was exhilarated but also scared
not of dying, of living through what lay ahead and after
And of the duty and joys of my command

Walked into combat knowing I might not make it out
Was okay with that for am a believer
Had the strength of faith in my troops, myself, and God

My body armor and my Lord's armor
always with me
Was a Christian in a foxhole

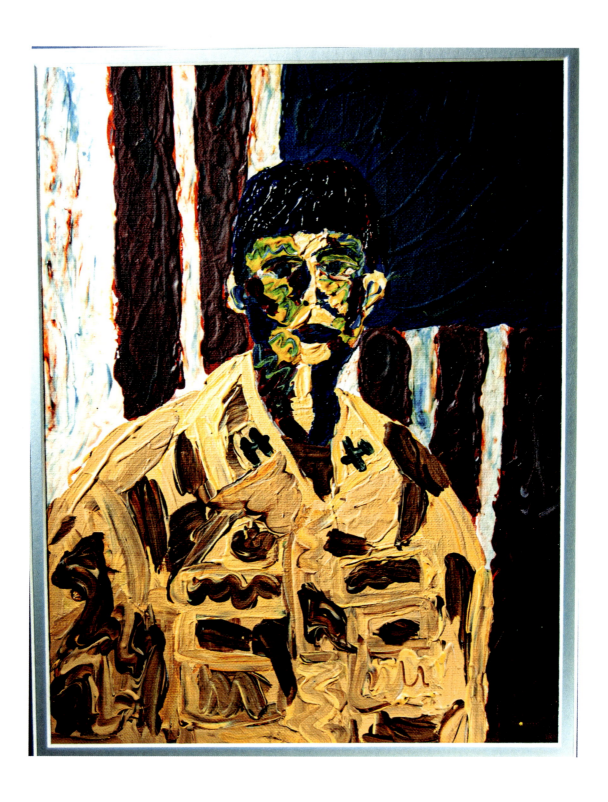

21. The Combat You

Combat changes you
There is the "you" before, then the "you" after
Both are forever altered and never the same post-combat

Even memories are different of the "you before"
Seemingly life was easier, like viewing the past through a soft filter
While memories of combat, of the "you after", are in vivid 3D, bloody and stained

Death was everywhere, you couldn't escape it then and cannot now
You lived and breathed it,
the sounds, smells, and sights are embedded into your brain.

Can still hear the cries of those seized by fear in the night
The stench of burning flesh comes back with a simple barbecue with friends
Explosively intense sight of a truck blown up by a suicide bomber stuck in my head

These are what the "you after" in me lives and struggles with
Images resurface when least expected, stunning, taking me from what is to what was
Powerful memories compete with reality.

Such young lives destroyed by IEDs, VBIEDs, small arms or mortar attacks
Cannot unsee what was seen or undo what was experienced
I keep moving forward, remembering to just breathe

Sometimes that is the best it gets
Just one breath at a time
One day at a time, one foot in front of the other.

22. Eye Fuckery

It starts with a glance
Seemingly innocent enough
but quickly develops into a cold, hard stare

Then transforms into the vilest of looks:
unwanted, leering, lewd, lecherous
The kind that strips you naked, leaving you exposed

My body armor couldn't protect me as I walked into the DFAC
Immediately sensed hundreds of eyes on me
All the men were starving, and I was the last piece of meat.

Was standing fully clothed but felt totally nude
Their eyes, lips, and gestures invaded my body without touching
Lingering on my breasts, my legs, my backside

No body part was exempt from the raw hunger
Desire oozed throughout their testosterone-fueled pores
I wanted to fight back, run out, scrub myself clean.

No way to do that, was in combat with a job to do
So, held my head high and used my own eyes and rank
to command those invading eyes to fuck off

Experienced lustful looks before, but never by hundreds
at the same time in a highly masculine combat environment
This was eye fuckery, just another hazard in the AOR.

23. Black Death

Black smoke oozed into pores
Penetrating unknowingly deep into lungs
Silently invading our bodies

Burn pits were everywhere
Spread out hundreds of feet high and wide
Freely emitting toxins

Little did we know
that each day of exposure
could bring illness or even death

Smokestacks burned 24/7
The enemy was inside the gates
A deadly chameleon smoldered among the ashes

Burn pits became a grim reaper
bringing disease and the black death
to many who served.

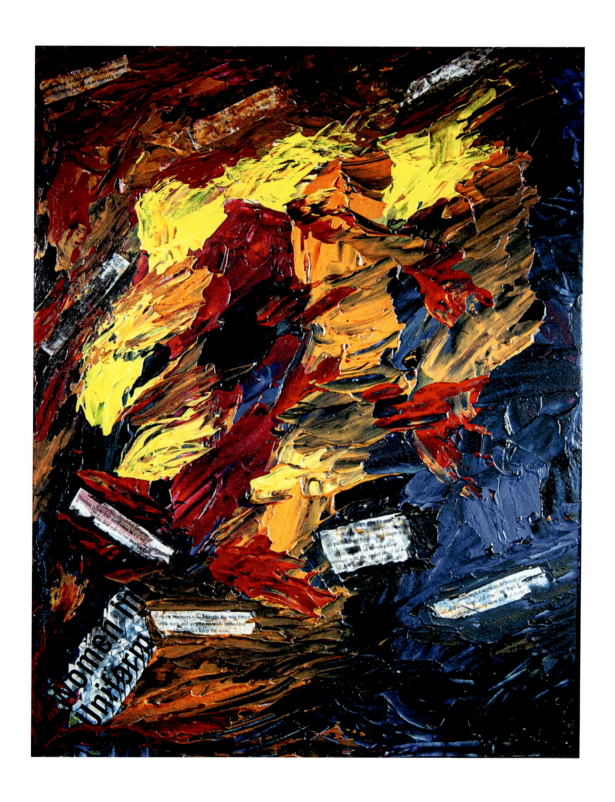

24. Echoes of War

We touched each other's war, decades apart
one in Vietnam, the other in Iraq
Sisters in arms, E-6 and O-6

Everywhere there were men
the leering, lecherous, catcalls nonstop
red meat to starving troops

Bloody shredded fatigues
Combat boots and uniforms laced with body parts
Sights that can never be unseen

Outgoing mortar fire
whirling of choppers overhead
The sounds of freedom as fighters, bombers soared

Incoming with things that go boom and kill
Small arms fire, rockets, mortars, grenades, IEDs
Brought fear and impending doom

Napalm and Agent Orange
and the toxic burn pits
all putrid, penetrating, and lingering

The stench of burning flesh
combined with the sweet smell of weed
didn't erase the odor of death

Women warriors who brought the war home
with seen and unseen wounds embedded
Our bodies keep the score

Although fought in different eras
we still see, hear, and smell the dark echoes of war
speaking, sharing now to heal those wounds.

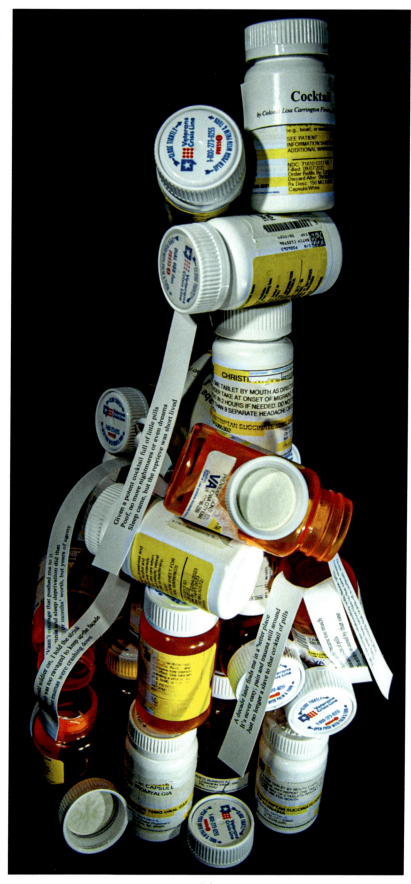

25. Cocktail

Humiliated, embarrassed,
reeking with shame
I crossed the threshold

Wasn't courage that pushed me to it
Insomnia and sleep deprivation did that
Not days or months' worth, but years of agony

My mind could soldier on, I told the shrink
But my body was too ravaged to keep up the façade
Years of past traumas were crashing down

Given a potent cocktail full of little pills
Poof, no more nightmares or even dreams
Sleep came, but the reprieve was short lived

The cocktail's side effects became too much
Buried under an avalanche of pills
This one for this that was caused by that one

Had a love-hate relationship with those pills
They went from savior-like to the new enemy
Had to knock that crutch of a cocktail away

A decade later finds me in a better place
It's never easy; pain and trauma still around
Just no longer a slave to that cocktail of pills

26. Command

Saluted smartly the white top's eagle license plate
Only a lieutenant, but knew at that precise moment I would command
that one day I would have a military car with an eagle

All my actions thereafter were in pursuit
of the intoxicating and powerful pull of command
Where others feared or were leery of command, I was drawn to it

Lots of people study leadership
Some even get to experience the application of it
Fewer still get the privilege of serving in actual command.

No other leadership role compares to being a military commander.
The challenges, frustrations, and sheer weight of responsibility
are both exhilarating and terrifying.

The duty of a leader who commands is never ending.
Their actions impact lives, the mission, and national security.
Always on 24/7, one must keep the power in check.

Being a commander is an honor and a privilege
A real test of one's leadership, perseverance, and grit
The best always put their troops first.

I worked hard every day as a commander
to not forget the sacrifices made by those that wear the uniform.
It was my troops who taught me what command is all about.

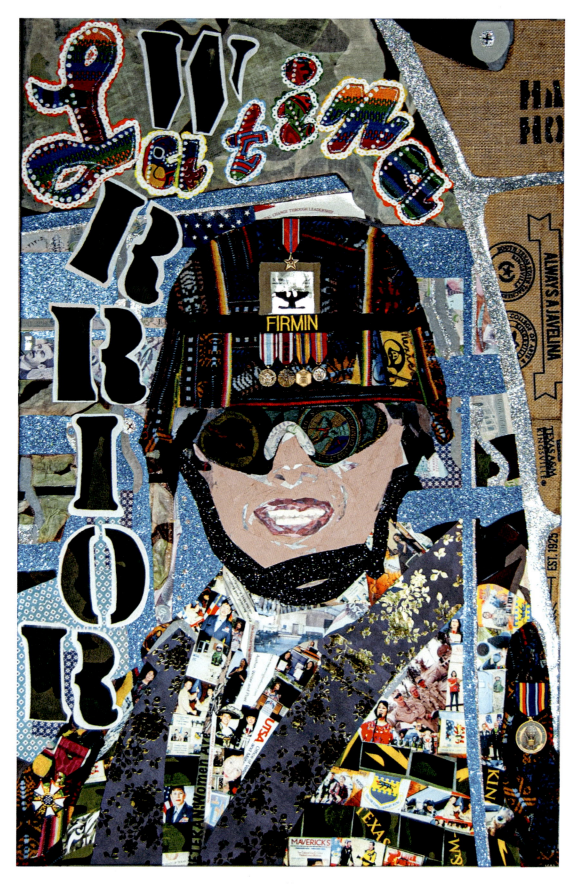

27. Guerrera Latina

Latina de nacimiento
Guerrera por propia elección
Sobreviviente por ganas
Llevo la sangre de mis antepasados

Latina de nacimiento
Seguí el camino más difícil
Abriendo paso para los demás
Emergí con desperfectos, pero poderosa

Guerrera por propia elección
Serví, me sacrifiqué y marcada me quedé
Mujer latina, una fuerza multiplicadora
Valientemente me convertí en La Coronela

Sobreviviente por ganas
Combatí contra el enemigo de mi país
Peleé contra el enemigo a mi lado
Luché contra el enemigo en mi interior

Llevo la sangre de mis antepasados
Mi gente es valiente y orgulloso
Una fuerza de la naturaleza que jamás se rinde
Su fuente de vida corre feroz en mis venas.

27. Latina Warrior

Latina by birth
Warrior by choice
Survivor by ganas
The blood of my ancestors in me

Latina by birth
Took the toughest path
Paved the way for others
Emerged flawed but powerful

Warrior by choice
Served, sacrificed, scarred
My Latinaness a force multiplier
Boldly became La Coronela

Survivor by ganas
Fought my country's enemy
Battled the enemy next to me
Wrestled with the enemy inside

The blood of my ancestors in me
My people are brave and proud
A force of nature that never quits
Their life source is fierce in my veins.

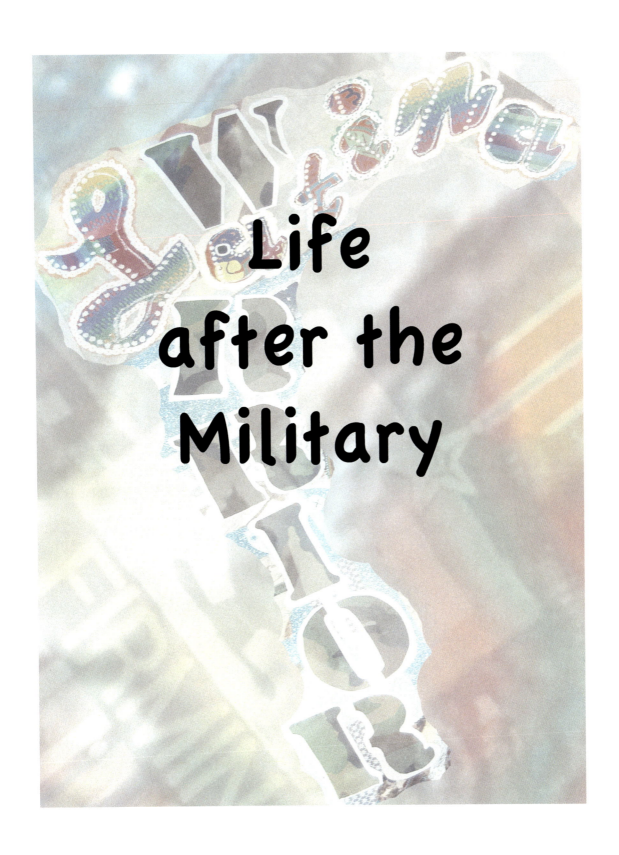

Life after the Military

Hung up the uniform after 30 years
and the world didn't stop or cease to exist
Life went on for me and everyone else

The easiest part of transition was confidence in myself
Wasn't intimidated, had led in peacetime and combat
Adapted and leveraged an extensive military skill set

I desperately missed the comfort of my combat boots
Wasn't prepared for the suffering that came with professional attire
How did women do this day in and day out?

The most painful and annoying aspect of transition
was figuring out what to wear every day
and in the civilian dress shoes I had to wear

I finally figured out the whole accessorizing thing!

28. Transition Blisters

Hung up the uniform after 30 years
and the world didn't stop or cease to exist
Life went on for me and everyone else

Was apprehensive and excited about the future
Didn't recognize the civilian staring back in the mirror
The hardest part was the immediate loss of identity

The easiest aspect of transition was confidence in myself
Wasn't intimidated, had led in peacetime and combat
Able to adapt and leverage an extensive military skill set

The most painful and annoying phase of transition
was figuring out what to wear every day
and experiencing civilian dress shoes

I desperately missed the comfort of my combat boots
No one prepared me for the suffering that came with professional attire
How did women do this day in and day out?

I had blisters on all my toes at the end of the first week
On the surface I exuded strength and was calm, cool, and collected
Underneath I was a pile of civilian clothes, accessories foreign to me

I had a new purpose, an important mission in higher education
But it took me months to feel comfortable on the inside
and to learn the vocabulary of the new world I had landed in

My leadership was rewarded by autonomy in all that I led and created
My second career was a perfect job match as it was a Hispanic Serving Institution
Helped others and finally figured out the whole accessorizing thing

29. Invisible Veteran

Do you see me?
You look beyond me and speak as if I am not even here
But I am standing right in front of you

Do you see me?
You acknowledge the male veteran next to me with your gratitude and respect
But you ignore my service and sacrifice

Do you see me?
You assume I'm someone's wife, daughter, sister, mother, or grandmother
But I served too

Do you see me?
You revert to your default setting that only men are warriors
But I am a combat veteran who is also a woman

Do you see me?
You downplay my contribution, unaware that women serve
But my sacrifice and valor were equal to or greater than some men

Do you see me?
You force me to work at gaining your respect
But haven't I already earned that?

Do you see me?
You still fail to identify or recognize me. I wonder if it is deliberate or ignorance
But my invisibility as a woman vet speaks volumes. Are you listening?

30. Superwoman Is Dead

I chased the dream for years
That elusive heady superpower of doing it all
Superwoman is dead

Did whatever was required by Uncle Sam
For family, others, and careers in higher education and as an entrepreneur
Superwoman is dead

Fought to be included
Then fought to not be as the cost became too high
Superwoman is dead

Proved Latinas and women could lead and excel
Family became second to the mission
Superwoman is dead

Forget work-life balance
Something always has to give
Superwoman is dead

Ended up with the wisdom
That taught me what was really important
Superwoman is dead

Overlook a dusty house and self-imposed deadlines
Work harder to ensure your family knows what they mean to you
Superwoman is dead

I fought for an unattainable goal
To exel at everything
Superwoman is dead

31. Save the Civilians

All it takes is a sight, sound, or smell
to take me right back there
to Commander mode in Iraq

Never know when it might come,
that thing that takes me there
to Commander mode in Iraq

Once it came while at the airport,
heard a sound that took me back
to Commander mode in Iraq

Heard rocket and mortar fire,
took me back, I was THERE
in Commander mode in Iraq

That combat fire was all too real,
back among my troops and the enemy
in Commander mode in Iraq

My heart raced, was hyper alert,
super focused, sweating and running
in Commander mode in Iraq

Screaming "Save the civilians!" in my head
'cause it's time to step up and lead again
in Commander mode in Iraq

Ran towards the sounds of combat,
to find it was bird shot that took me back
to Commander mode in Iraq

32. The Sisterhood

I am a woman veteran, part of an awesome Sisterhood
that is very much alive and well,
diverse and prospering with every lived experience shared

This vibrant and living tribe
envelopes me like a warm, cozy quilt from Quilts of Honor
Uniting US, validating and honoring common service and sacrifice

The Sisterhood is like a retreat for my soul
allowing me a safe space like the Military Women's Memorial
to be authentic, to unburden my pain, to feel again

The clan accepts me as is. I am both honored and humbled,
no judgement found among the Sisterhood
just acceptance, forgiveness, love, and understanding

When I meet a sister vet,
I am no longer alone and reignite with inspiration and empowerment.
Nothing is impossible, I am ten feet tall and bulletproof.

Don't tread on the Sisterhood. We are powerful,
growing in numbers every day. Make way, we are here to stay.
Hear us roar, feel our strength, we are the Sisterhood.

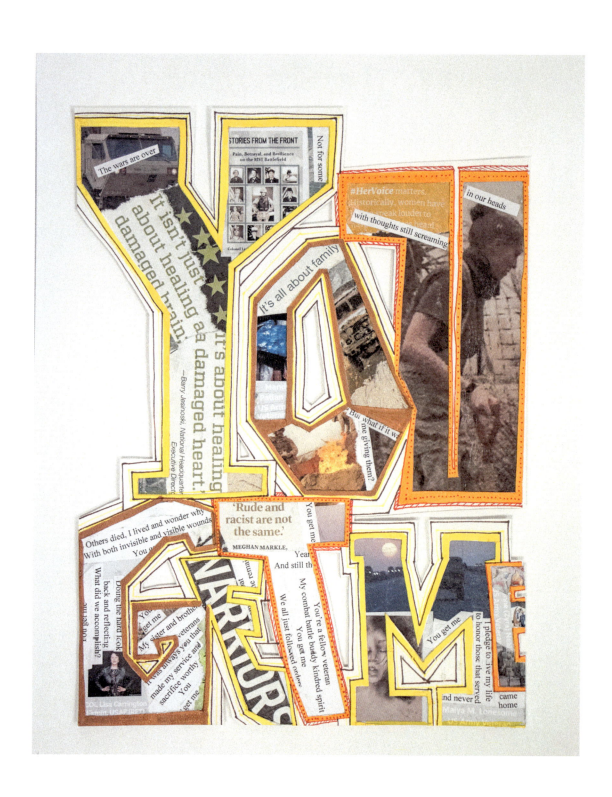

33. You Get Me

You're a fellow veteran
My combat battle buddy kindred spirit
You get me

Years removed from combat
And still the guilt and self-blame remain
You get me

We all just followed orders
But what if it was me giving them?
You get me

Others died, I lived and wonder why
With both invisible and visible wounds
You get me

The wars are over
Not for some, with thoughts still screaming in our heads
You get me

Doing the hard look back and reflecting
What did we accomplish?
You get me

I pledge to live my life
to honor those that served and never came home
You get me

My sister and brother veterans
It was always you that made my service and sacrifice worthy
You get me

34. Get Out of My Head

I am not crazy
Are you sure you don't hear it?
That buzzing, ringing noise

Once I tore the entire house apart
Searching for that incessant noise
My brain kept screaming it was everywhere

Went from room to room
Checked all lights and electrical gadgets
Even went outside and explored the streetlight

The buzzing stayed the same
No matter where I went or what I did
Never abated. How can that be?

I shouted GET OUT OF MY HEAD
Because that's where it was
That piercing, ringing radio static

I thought I was losing my mind trying to find quiet
It is so LOUD, like a chicharra rock concert
Ruptured a blood vessel in my eye blowing out the noise from my ears

I am not crazy
You just can't hear it
It's IN my head between my ears

I can't turn it off
It is always with me
The best I can do is try to ratchet it down

Of all my itises, this tinnitus is the most annoying
Because no one else is in my head
Just this ear-piercing, shrill noise and me.

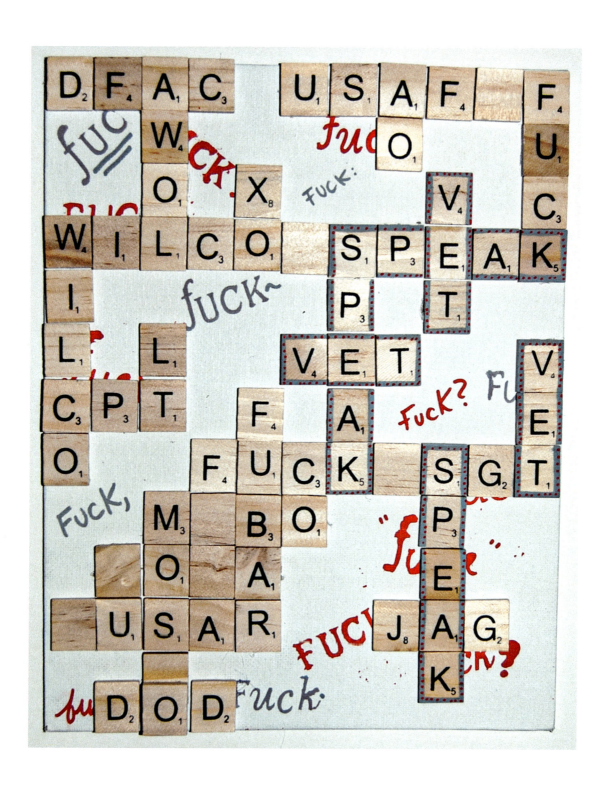

35. VetSpeak

Dad used to tell me that my mouth would get me into trouble
He should know, he was a sailor AND an airman
and I've always been my father's daughter

Every so often I am known to use colorful language
Usually intensifies when among my fellow vets
The most creative use was in combat

Sort of like a no holds barred lingo
that can indicate meaning rapidly and concisely
Quite efficient when time is of the essence

This type of language is simply one dialect of VetSpeak
full of acronyms; shorthand for people, places, things, and war stories
A word or two can bring instant meaning and camaraderie

Take the word fuck
Does it mean the act itself, a good thing, a bad thing, or what?
It can mean all that or nothing at all

It can just be a filler
A conversation pause or an exclamation mark
Can convey excitement, happiness, anger, or contempt

Once while engaged in conversation with several vets
Noticed a few frequently used the word fuck indiscrimately
No obvious sentiment was noted

That particular word was being used as a gap
in the ongoing conversation, nothing else, nothing more
Fuck was just a comma

Death of a Wife

She loved him
For years
Until she didn't.

Cannot pinpoint when,
The exact day or even year
The wife in her died.

Never saw it coming
Was a slow, gradual process,
Like a deadly disease that kills so slowly

She mourned the loss of the man she married.
The one she thought she truly loved,
Not the man she divorced.

Did she ever really know him?
Was he the chameleon
Or was she?

The wife in her died long before the split.
She stoically attended the wake.
Then totally rocked the Celebration of life.

36. Death of a Wife

She loved him
for years
Until she didn't

Cannot pinpoint when,
the exact day or even year
The wife in her died

Never saw it coming
Was a slow, gradual process,
like a deadly disease that kills slowly

She mourned the loss of the man she married
The one she thought she truly loved,
not the man she divorced

Did she ever really know him?
Was he the chameleon
Or was she?

The wife in her died long before the split
She stoically attended the wake
Then totally rocked the celebration of life

37. Death of a Marriage

Married her high school boyfriend when she was young,
the adventuresome one who made her laugh
Was happy for some time

The birth of a child brought contentment
Motherhood and the military consumed her daily existence
Left in third place was the marriage

Soon the laughter faded away into silence
Easier to ignore than confront, tolerate than face, settle than live
The marriage started to decay

Began to smell unpleasant like a rotten corpse
The signs were all around her, in every aspect of her life,
but still she didn't quit or leave

She wonders why it took so long
to realize the marriage was gone, had flatlined years before,
that life support couldn't save it

The death of the marriage untethered the ball and chain
No more pretending she was happy
Free at last to be who she was destined to be, to really live

Earned my place and scars
as a leader, author, and poet
I KNOW THAT,
so why do I at times feel like
I don't belong?

38. Not an Imposter

The wrong gender for the military
Not Mexican enough for the Latinos
Too ethnic for the gringos

Worked hard to get here
To fit in whatever space I find myself
So why do I sometimes feel I don't belong?

That sense of being out of place
still occasionally rears its ugly head
discounting any success achieved

Believe my Spanish is just not good enough
Feel trapped in the space between cultures
Then find myself traversing both with ease

Recall feeling inferior to fellow officers
from Ivy league colleges or academies
then outscoring them in military schools

Doubted myself as an author
and the depth and significance of what I took on
My publisher quickly expelled those thoughts

Am I really a poet? How many poems equal a poet?
Can clearly hear that imposter voice taunting me right now
Took others stating emphatically that I was a poet before I could

Earned my place and scars as a leader, author, and poet
I know that, so why do I sometimes feel I don't belong?

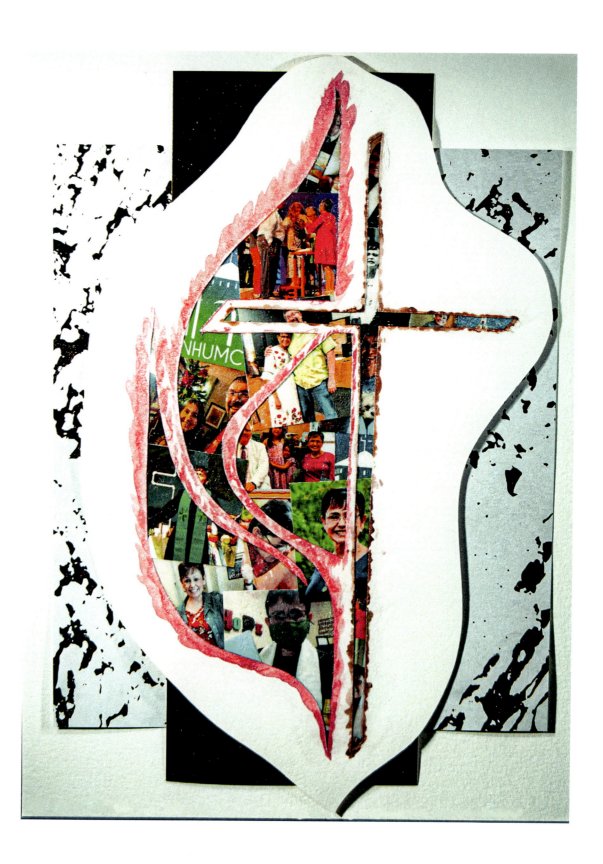

39. Mi Pastora

She's a rockstar for Jesus
Touched by the Holy Spirit
The Lord whisperer

Reaches and peers deep into souls
Shares her direct line to God with all
Fuerte, friendly and so very kind

Teaches and radically shares the Word
La metodista moves others with her sermons
Translates biblical messages into present day

Loves with compassion and intentionality
Fiercely helps others grow in Christ
Like a love beacon in a dark world

The Lord blessed me when we met
Had never seen a pastor who looked like me
A true inspiration for this Latina

She is mi pastora
A leader, preacher, and powerful role model
The light shines bright in her

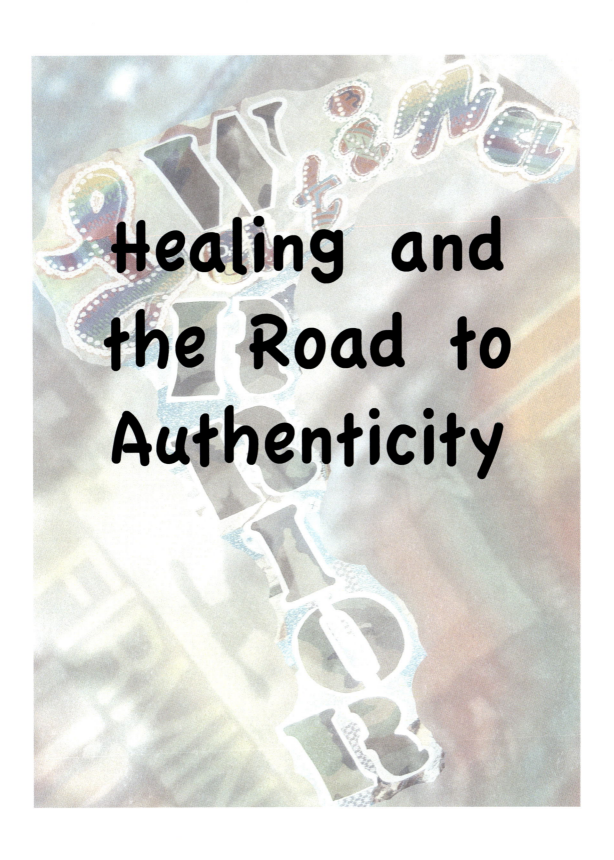

Healing and the Road to Authenticity

40. Into the Light

While the world raged against a pandemic in 2020, the first in 100 years,
> I raged against a virulent strain of testosterone filled traumas.

While the country masked up and used sanitizer to keep the virus at bay,
> I lifted the mask that hid years of sexual harassment while serving my country.

While the nation underwent lockdowns and faced months of darkness to protect its citizens from the virus,
> I came into the light, face to face with the betrayals of my brothers in arms.

While scientists researched innovative new vaccines,
> I reflected on my past military time serving alongside both professionals and hidden predators, and researched ways to heal.

While businesses tried to keep people six feet apart to be safe,
> I began learning how to let people in, closer to a heart and body that is guarded.

While most were wary and complained about isolation and quarantine,
> I felt safe hunkered down alone.

While I missed my family terribly,
> I used the lockdown and self-isolation to begin the long road of healing that had eluded me in the past.

While some courageously spoke openly about military sexual trauma,
> I could not do that until one day in 2020, after a young Army Specialist was found brutally murdered on a military base.

While Vanessa Guillén anguished over reporting her sexual harassment and the retaliation it might bring,
> I understood all too well the trepidation and fear of what reporting my own could have brought.

While Vanessa's death astounded the country,
> I was affected deep into my Latina soul, and her murder became a catalyst to acknowledge my own bitter truth.

While Vanessa's family mourned and demanded answers from an inept military,
> I found my voice from their tragic loss.

While the investigation into her murder revealed serious gaps within the military,
> I discovered my own repressed memories.

While sexually assaulted in initial training,
> I froze, tolerating more than anyone should ever have to.

While relentlessly harassed early in my career,
> I will not allow those early years to define me. I am a leader, a woman, a Latina, a combat warrior, my bronze star shines bright.

While other voices cry out for change within the Armed Services,
> I join them, my mask now lifted, and walk into the light.

41. MST Warrior

I am a Military Sexual Trauma warrior
Never a victim, much more than a survivor
Owning my past jettisons me into a present and future worthy of happiness

MST happened to me, without my permission or consent
It didn't matter what I wore, how much I might have drunk
The power differential was huge, I was young, vulnerable, a nobody

Overpowered and betrayed by someone I trusted and respected
A predator took advantage, exploited my weaknesses
with no regard for my humanity

I know now it was about power not sex
MST rests alongside my pain, guilt, and shame, haunting me
But resilience emerges the strongest of them all

Astounded at how many fellow MST Warriors are out there like me
Their strength and courage embolden me on a journey of healing and advocacy
Can no longer sit idly by, am compelled to act

MST Warriors everywhere cry out for justice and change
Every lived experience shared brings vulnerability AND empowerment
Our stories are important.
One is powerful; combined they blend like a commanding tsunami

Sharing my story and others to make a difference on the MST Battlefield
Not broken, but beautifully crafted to emerge stronger after trauma
For I am an MST Warrior.

42. The Grunt and the Colonel

Two women warriors, both Texas gals
Fought in wars decades apart
In the Far East and the Middle East

Prepared to die in faraway lands
Tough and hardened by combat and life
Left part of themselves in Vietnam and Iraq

Stood up for the USA and fought
Took the oath to support and defend
Did not shy away from duty, honor, and country

Heckled for wars they did not start
One welcomed by protestors
The other like a heroine

Two tortured souls on the same healing journey
Came home with invisible wounds
PTSD unites them, but does not define them

Past traumas and combat experiences
Now honestly and openly discussed
The women warriors serve as lifelines for each other

One enlisted, one officer; part of the sisterhood
Overcame, survived, and thrived
Their Bronze Stars share only one part of their story

Fate brought them together
Service and sacrifice will forever bind them
The Grunt and the Colonel helping each other heal

43. La Rona/The Trickster

She goes by many names:
SARS-CoV-2, Corona, Covid-19
I just call her La Rona, The Trickster

She's been a harbinger of death and devastation
Still causing immense suffering to so many
Cannot underestimate her evil ways

Almost three years into a worldwide pandemic
She slid stealthily into my home and body
Beaming like a gift-wrapped holiday present

Each day brought new ways to ravage my mind and form
Ever The Trickster, La Rona
steals hope and wreaks chaos on my healing

Even the very strong can falter
She has multiple faces, showing different sides of her treachery
Tricks me, lets me think I am beating her

Then strikes like a most formidable foe, slamming down another symptom
Bestowing me with yet another gift during a holiday without my family
Her toxicity lingers and leaves a chalky taste

The fatigue and brain fog come and go
I take one step forward and three back, energy reserves deplete rapidly
Hard to focus on any one thing too long with this super amped brain on fire

Despite strong feelings of despair I experience daily
I know just how blessed I really am
Lifelines in the form of goodwill, prayer, food, and strength come steadily in

Marching time with La Rona, The Trickster
Writing her as the loser here, for I am not giving up or giving in
This Latina still has a lot of living to do, my work is not yet done.

44. Fractured

I see fragments of my sexual assault
bits and pieces that are fleeting
Memories floating loosely around in my head

It's like trying to watch a movie,
a really old brittle super 8mm one
with so many splices and cuts

Simply impossible to watch
from beginning to end,
so many breaks, gaps, and broken seams

Cannot grasp the missing pieces
They slip through so easily,
elusively obscure in my mind

What's left are fractured shards
I try hard to retain every twisted detail
But the blurred bits are never clear enough

I don't remember everything he did to me
It's scary not to know, not to recall each painful part
And, it's even scarier that I might remember it all

To know each excruciating moment would break me
Being fractured keeps me whole.

45. The Abyss

It is not a safe haven
More like an open chest wound that is bleeding out
You feel your very existence draining away

Facing demons of PTSD and MST
Thrust me into The Abyss, the black hole of life
The fragile space between fully living and just existing

I cannot allow myself to stay here
In the dark recesses of my splintered mind
Where pain, fear, guilt, and shame lie

Intense memories of trauma drag me down even deeper
I cannot escape that seductive siren call from the pitch-black void
It whispers just how much easier it would be to succumb

Trying to reconcile the past and the present with my future
Without losing myself permanently in The Abyss
Must fight to break the hold it has on me

The war continues in my head, heart, and soul
Some battles I win, others The Abyss screams it is the victor
Time will tell the final outcome

I will never give up fighting for my sanity
To exist, to live fully in the light, to be whole. For I know I am worthy
The Abyss will not take me down, it cannot win.

You left
Abadoned me
Jilted, dejected
ANGRY, cast aside
Scared, you're really gone
Am hurt, the separation weighs heavy on me

You knew the real me
Dropped my guard and let you in
My deepest, darkest secrets shared
Grateful for our time spent together
I trusted you and understood why you left
But THE BREAKUP still hurts

You helped me see what I couldn't
Confided in you,
now comfortable
with vulnerability
Learned, grew,
and built my own
survival toolkit

Abandoned
but not alone
Emerged stronger
after trauma
Empowered after therapy

The right one at the right time
relationship, left me better equipped to face my demons

46. The Breakup

You left
Abandoned me
Jilted, dejected

Angry, cast aside
Scared, you're really gone
Am hurt, the separation weighs heavy on me

You knew the real me
Dropped my guard and let you in
My deepest, darkest secrets shared

Grateful for our time spent together
I trusted you and understood why you left
But the breakup still hurts

You helped me see what I couldn't
Confided in you, now comfortable with vulnerability
Learned, grew, and built my own survival toolkit

Abandoned but not alone
Emerged stronger after trauma
Empowered after therapy

You were my therapist
The right one at the right time
Our "relationship" left me better equipped to face my demons.

47. Pain

Awake to pain
Physical and emotional
Thank the Lord can still feel

Pain travels from my head to my feet
Ants with sledgehammers crawl and pummel over my body
Nerves, muscles, joints on fire

People look at me and think all is well
They have no idea what lurks beneath the surface
Some days I can pass as okay

Others not so much
Rage, guilt, shame from trauma catch up to the physical pain
Making it hard to breathe as my head and body are ablaze together

It's a constant fight
Easier to give in, take shots of bourbon, pills, and steroids
But not my SOP. The control freak in me treads lightly, I need to be in charge

Irritable, so very tired
Some days just want to be alone and wallow in it all
I cling to my pain like a lover

For who would I be without pain?
Don't think I can handle knowing, not sure I deserve it
Desolation sets in so effortlessly

The cycle keeps repeating
Pain becomes an angry, pissed-off roommate that just never leaves
Crushing, pressing down on me. The battle continues

Each day is a gift
It's what I choose to do with it that matters
I take full advantage of the good days.

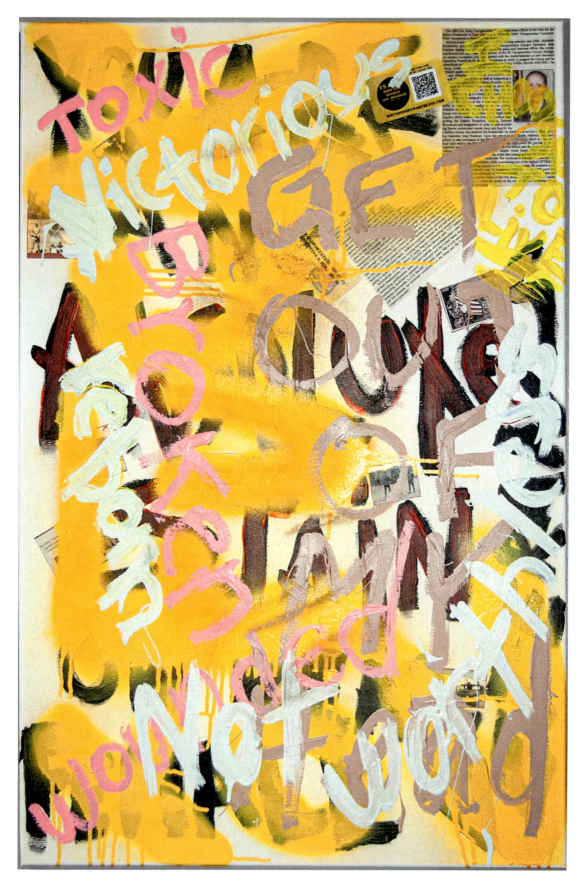

48. Wounded Not Worthless

Fuck you!
Am still here
You did not win

Glimpses of battles
Already fought
You were my LIMFAC

Journey fraught
With physical and emotional pain
You made the struggle worse

PTSD, MST and all the toxic characters
Visible and invisible
You kept me fractured, never whole

Broken and shattered
Now reborn and reinvigorated and yet,
You resurface once again slithering like a snake

Get out of my head
My splintered FUBAR psyche
You no longer rent space in my consciousness

Wounded not worthless
Deeply scarred but victorious
You can crawl back into your hole. I choose to live.

49. Life

I lament
        Linger
        Languish
But most of all I linger

I listen
        Learn
        Lead
But most of all I learn

I laugh
        Live
        Love
But most of all I live

50. Writing Is My Salvation

Years of unaddressed trauma
Was slowly killing me inside
Like a thousand sharply aimed cuts

Summoned the courage to face my demons
They had frolicked without restraint in my head far too long
We went at it, demons and Latina, fisticuffs and all

Would have been easier to give up, so very painful
Didn't give in, stuck with it and beat the crap out of them
Tamed what had been attacking me stealthily for years

Therapy, talking with vets, writing, poetry and artistic collaboration
are all aspects of my healing, but writing emerged as the most powerful
No longer ashamed, vibrantly liberated to be my authentic self

With every word I write, every poem I pen, the burden lessens
Am taking back my past and owning it as a permanent part of me
Now am free to abate that death of a thousand cuts, one word at a time

Learned the hard way that I am the best narrator of my own experiences
The Lord blessed me, am just the vessel as a writer and a storyteller
Our stories matter, sharing them helps others as well as ourselves.

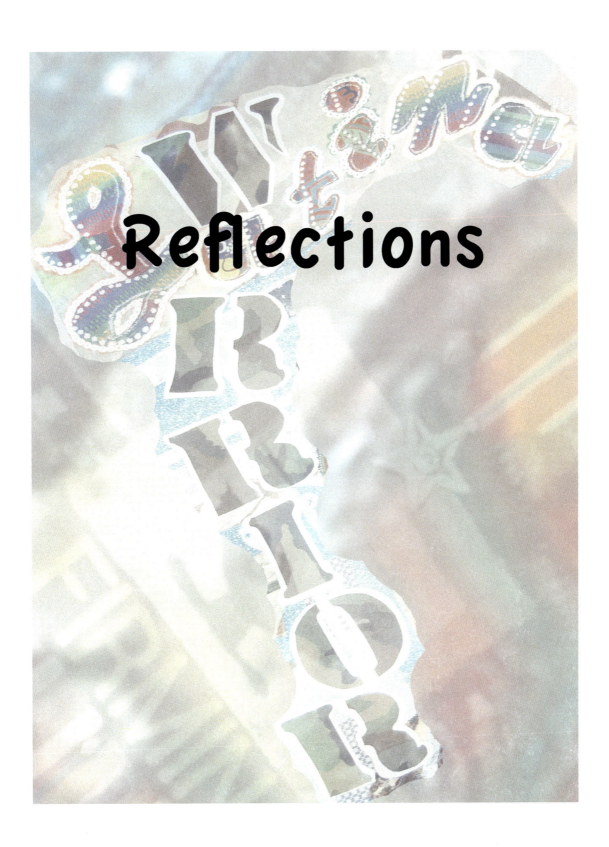

Early Years y Familia

1. Globetrotter

Poet:

I was privileged to grow up all over the world due to my father's military service. I didn't realize until I was older just how special that really was. Learning that differences could be both honored and celebrated taught me valuable lessons about inclusion that have stayed with me. "Globetrotter" was written to capture that vagabond lifestyle that instilled many life lessons and the respect of others on a global scale. I wasn't sure how Christina was going to create this piece. I wanted to somehow depict where I lived during my childhood, so I sent her pictures of items that represented where I had lived and the result was really cool.

Artist:

"Globetrotter" is a 12" x 12" traditional mixed media collage made up of several varieties of acid-free papers. I was inspired to create this piece from the second-to-last stanza about the "connective tissue," which I collaged directly onto the work. Lisa also sent me pictures of places she grew up in as a military dependent, so I was able to draw directly from her rich background as well.

2. Big Bro

Poet:

Growing up with an older brother was both difficult and satisfying. I certainly went through the love/hate stage, and as time went by began to realize and appreciate that I had been taught many lessons along the way. "Big Bro" captures much of my early experiences with an older brother, one I fiercely competed with, loved, and hated at the same time. It took me years to realize that I was blessed to grow up with him and my younger siblings. For the art, I was asked to provide only one picture but ended up giving Christina more than that. The one she used really epitomizes my relationship with my older brother.

Artist:

"Big Bro" is a pencil sketch on an organically-shaped 8"x 10" piece of vellum. I created this piece from a black-and-white photograph that Lisa sent me after I asked her for the one photograph that encapsulated her relationship with her big brother. I drew it with a soft lead pencil on this translucent delicate substrate to highlight all the subtle clashes happening in the poem. Here, along the thoughtful torn edges of the paper, you will find the two siblings posing for another holiday photo, already fading like our memories, yet still somehow substantial because of its inelegance.

3. Flaca

Poet:

I had many nicknames bestowed upon me by loving relatives. The names themselves at times were not so loving but were given con mucho cariño. The one that has stuck with me to this day is behind my poem "Flaca." It took me a while to realize that the nicknames were terms of endearment. There is a flaco/flaca in every Latino family. Perhaps you will think of the one in yours when you read about my experience. I love this piece! I wanted it to be whimsical, and Christina delivered.

Artist:

"Flaca" is a 5"x 7" watercolor pen and ink painting. Lisa told me that flaca means skinny and was one of her many nicknames growing up—so I could just "draw a tall bean pole with glasses with big balls, ha, that was me." I'm not sure if she thought I'd take her literally lol! But this is the final iteration of what we came up with. The first few were too sexy (can a bean pole be too sexy? Yes, yes it can—think too long legs with high heels) or the hair was not quite right. There really is a precise way to hit the target with string bean watercolor.

4. La Manguera

Poet:

Who knew that a simple garden hose would prompt a poem many years later? I was drawn to the simplicity of "La Manguera" which conveys exactly how we kids played outside all the time and weren't really allowed inside until it was dinner time. It didn't matter to us that it tasted like rubber and was hot. That coiled snake provided us the sustenance to continue our play. This poem signifies for me a simpler time.

Artist:

"La Manguera" is a 5" x 7" mixed media watercolor collage. This is a quick pencil sketch and watercolor painting of an old garden hose as I would have imagined in the backyard of the author in one of her homes growing up. No bottled water for her, she said. She spent most of her time outdoors doing all kinds of sports and activities, and the one constant was the old trusty manguera (hose). I also used an acrylic skin medium process for the words, so as to give it a more antiquated look to go along with the old garden hose painting. To finish the piece, I found a worn vintage frame at the local antique shop that was a perfect fit.

5. First Gen

Poet:

My ganas kicked in during my college years: that desire, ambition, and drive to get ahead, to make something of myself. It truly became my superpower. Being a first-generation college student was not an easy path, but I embraced it. I dreamed of being the first in my family to graduate and make them all proud. "First Gen" captures my experiences at Texas A&I University (now known as Texas A&M University-Kingsville), and I am hopeful that it can inspire others to stay the course so that they too, can change the trajectories of their lives.

Artist:

"First Gen" is an 11" x 14" mixed media watercolor collage inspired by the idea that Lisa's superpower was her ganas. I took that concept and used a generic superhero emblem as the base for a collage window into what would keep our hero going all those years "despite feeling totally like an outsider." As she put on her cape and proudly wore her First Gen badge, she had the love and support of her family as well as her new Javelina Nation friends.

6. In the Bleachers

Poet:

The reflective journey that inspired *Latina Warrior* allowed me to look deep into my past and to appreciate the childhood that I was so fortunate to have. "In the Bleachers" was a way for me to pay homage to my father, a selfless man who pushed us hard to be the best that each of us could be. He served in both the Navy and the Air Force. I desperately wanted his respect and tried extremely hard to earn it. He supported all my endeavors, but none more so than the sports I engaged in. Rain or shine, he would be there to cheer me on in victory and defeat, all the while demonstrating through his actions so many life lessons. My Latino father never put any restrictions on me, gender or otherwise. He encouraged me to dream big and to go for life with gusto. I teared up when I saw the art that Christina created; it was as if my father was back larger than life. Her idea for a postcard on this piece was genius.

Artist:

"In the Bleachers" is an 11" x 14" mixed media collage made from an assorted mix of acid-free papers inspired by Lisa's father. Lisa sent me some extremely precious photos of her father from when he was in the miliary, as well as one of her and him together. I then had the idea of creating a postcard in the piece, because when I read the poem, I got the impression that it was almost like I was reading a private correspondence that I had accidentally picked up—and I was now somehow blessed with dropping it off in the mail so it could finally reach the intended recipient. I collaged everything together and had my own dad create a custom frame to finish the piece off in a distinctive hard wood.

7. Tomasita

Poet:

"Tomasita" conveys the deep respect and love that I have for my mother. I wanted both to honor her and to demonstrate how strong many Latina matriarchs are, how they take on so much, fulfill multiple roles in the household, so that la familia can survive and flourish. My mom set the bar very high for all of us that followed. Her legacy lives on in me and others, and I continue to try to live my life so she would have been proud. On this earth my mother was the best of humanity. In heaven, I imagine she is happily dancing to Tejano music with my father. I sent Christina so many pictures of my mother with her children, grandchildren and great-grandchildren. I really wanted the art piece to depict the selfless love my mother had for her family and others. This piece came out exactly as I had envisioned. It brings me great joy and is a wonderful partner to accompany my poem.

Artist:

"Tomasita" is a 12" x 12" mixed media collage in a hand-crafted solid oak frame custom made by my father. This was one of the few poems about which Lisa had a specific view of how she would like it illustrated because it was about her mom, a "spiritual rockstar," someone who was truly selfless. I cannot tell you how many emails I got with pictures of children, grandchildren, even great-grandchildren. There were so many pictures inspired by this amazing woman! It was so hard to choose, to be sure, and Lisa thought praying hands would be the most elegant way to symbolize her mother, with the love of all her family shining through them. I was able to have my own father custom make a frame from solid oak to completely encapsulate this image. I then used acid-free papers and bunches of flowers and hearts and butterflies (symbolizing life, beauty, rebirth, and love) along the four corners.

8. Valley Girl

Poet:

"Valley Girl" is my attempt to pay tribute to my fondest memories of la familia in the South Texas valley region. Not quite sure how my father was able to arrange his military assignments, but he always managed to have a tour in Texas before and after an overseas one. This allowed us to spend many a summer or special occasion with the larger extended family, of which there are many. I may have lived abroad and far away, but I know where my roots are: in el valle. I thought Christina was able to capture the essence of the poem in her art. Look closely and you will see mi gente and all things valle.

Artist:

"Valley Girl" is an 8" x 10" traditional mixed media collage. Lisa sent me many pictures of her growing up all around the Rio Grande Valley in South Texas. Celebrating her culture and her family was very important to her father, so he always made sure they spent long vacations there every year. I layered the pictures of the traditional collage with the acrylic skin medium technique on top, with the words in differing levels of translucency. I also found a teal wooden frame that highlighted many of the colors present in the collaged pictures to finish off the piece nicely.

9. Javelinas

Poet:

I didn't realize until years after I graduated just how significant my time at Texas A&I University (now known as Texas A&M University-Kingsville) really was in shaping my educational foundation and cementing my never-ending pursuit of knowledge. In "Javelinas" I wanted to state unequivocally that all alumni of this fine institution are Javelinas and of one huge network. I am proud to give back with my leadership, my art, and my gifts. Establishing a scholarship at my alma mater was a significant milestone for me in helping others to achieve their own dreams. I totally love the art piece for "Javelinas," as it pays tribute to the heritage of the institution and symbolizes my view of todos somos Javelinas. The mascot looks ferocious; Christina nailed it!

Artist:

"Javelinas" is a 48" x 36" acrylic painting illustrating the idea that it "doesn't matter when you graduated or if you are A&I or TAMUK—Somos Javelinas!" Lisa sent me several ideas, and I even completed a small 5"x 7" watercolor piece for her after my initial read on this piece, but her initial feedback was basically, "Bigger. We have to go much bigger!"

We had many sessions after that preliminary sit-down, but one thing was clear: I needed to get across the notion of "We are one institution, una cultura" in some way. We settled on trying to combine the many different and/or former Javelina colleges using T-shirts, gathering up under the one mighty Javelina mascot symbolically rendered in the twilight Texas sky. I painted the piece using palette knives and coarse-haired brushes strategically using the school's colors and hues throughout the entire work.

10. Home

Poet:

My second assignment in the military found me in the Philippines, far from home. I missed everything about home, especially my mother's cooking and the fellowship from la familia. "Home" really honors my culture and the importance of passing down the customs of how certain foods are made and shared.

Making tamales is a tradition in my family and can be an art form. The smells of tamales cooking warm my heart and comfort me deep down into my soul. The powerful flood of memories and family come together in just one bite. I am honored that I can continue the tamale-making tradition.

For the art, I sent Christina bags of corn husks as she was thinking of creating a sculpture of some kind. I wasn't sure what she had in mind, but the final piece is outstanding. The brightly colored ojas authentically speak to the sentiment behind my words for "Home."

Artist:

"Home" is a 21" x 30" mixed media sculpture created out of corn husks, Rit fabric dye, a tabletop wreath stand, paper, Southwest pottery, and silk flowers. I learned how to brightly dye tamale corn husks over a three-day period in order to glue them to a double wreath stand in an alternating fashion. Once done, I found a coordinating pot of silk flowers to fit in the center of the wreath stand that could hold the final stanza of the poem.

11. The Boy, The Man, and The Father

Poet:

I decided one Father's Day to gift my son a poem about how much he meant to me and how proud I was of the man and father that he had become. It was also important for me to tell him just how sorry I was for when I couldn't be present during his childhood due to military duties. Growing up in a military family can require much sacrifice and be quite difficult on children. I had guilt due to my absences and knew that he had been affected by them.

As I look at my son, I can see in a split second all the various stages of his life almost all at once. I wonder if all mothers do that? I only know that, for me, it fuels my thirsting heart each and every day. I ended up writing "The Boy, The Man, and The Father" in the wee hours of one Father's Day morning. I think it was the best gift I could have given us both that day.

Artist:

"The Boy, The Man, and The Father" is a 12" x 12" collage paying homage to Lisa's son, from baby to man and all the stops in between. It is a pictorial love letter from a professional working mother to her son—layering all her struggles and love with her regrets and tender devotion. It is hard to see in a 2D presentation, but this piece has three different levels (three distinct layers that the pictures are raised up to), giving the work depth at each stop—with the poem's lines interjected at different spots along the way.

12. Mis Amigas

Poet:

Many of us have a core group of friends or family that are the bedrock of support and encouragement for us. "Mis Amigas" was written to pay respect to the many strong women in both my personal and my professional life. I have been able to endure and overcome much due to their unwavering support, advice, and love over many years. I will be forever grateful to them. Christina's rendition of "Mis Amigas" is great. It truly captures my deepest love and respect for these fierce women.

Artist:

"Mis Amigas" is a 16" x 20" mixed media collage I created from acrylic skins, matte acrylic medium, acrylic paint, and acid-free paper. The process for this piece involved receiving several emails filled with cherished photographs from Lisa that held her amigas, her superstars as she called them, the ones that supported her no matter what. First, I made a conventional collage of photographs to begin the piece, on top of a base matte of deep sunflower yellow. Then, on top of those layers, I carefully painted the rough outlined image of Lisa in her 'command' pose and filled it in with acrylic skins that I made from more of her treasured photographs. The final effect is a translucent figure created from and surrounded by all those "allies, advocates, and amplifiers"!

13. Bear

Poet:

My one-eyed long-haired dachshund was much more than a companion. "Bear" captures the essence of who and what he was. He emitted so much joy, strength, and compassion. Our bond was strong. It was as if he rose to every challenge that life threw at me, while I tried to rise to the challenges that he faced as well. We made quite a team and traveled frequently together. His passing left a huge void but helped to create the spark I needed to commence an intense healing journey on multiple levels. It's almost like that was his intent for me, and his passing occurred exactly when it did for that very reason. Christina brought to life my idea for this art. It's perfect.

Artist:

"Bear" is a 9" by 12" mixed media collage made with charcoal, pen/ink, and assorted acid-free papers. This piece speaks to the true connection that Lisa had with her dachshund Bear. I didn't get a lot of *directed* guidance with many of my pieces, but Lisa was *really* particular with this one. She sent specific pictures of her with him, and then she sent over a picture of a paw print of "LOVE" and asked if I could somehow create pictures of them together in it. Of course I could, it was for Bear! Hopefully I was able to meet her expectations, because you can really tell how much she loves her dog, not just in her words, but by her actions.

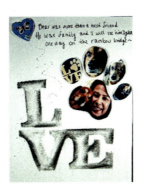

14. Ay Mijita

Poet:

"Ay Mijita" captures one of those moments in your life when, looking back, you know you could have handled it better from the onset. I put my role in the military first and foremost and forgot just for a moment what it would be like for a mother to hear that her daughter was going into harm's way. Am actually glad that my mother reacted the way she did. It reminded me of what countless other family members must have been going through, and grounded me for my command tour in Iraq. I could never forget that no matter what, we were talking about the sons, daughters, husbands, wives of others. I thought the art for this poem was quite creative and spot on. Really am enthralled with how Christina's imagination is so diverse.

Artist:

"Ay Mijita" is an 8" x 10" mixed media watercolor collage I created from paper, peel-and-stick tiles, a pencil sketch, and watercolor paint. After reading the poem and then speaking with Lisa about it, I felt there were three major ideas I wanted to express in this illustration: 1) that Lisa's mother had a real fear of her daughter going to war, 2) that her mother also had a real fear of losing her mijita, and 3) that Lisa could significantly feel her mother's love and prayers every day while deployed.

I decided the way I could depict "Ay Mijita" graphically was by recreating the Sunni Triangle space that Lisa was deployed to by outlining the area in heavy tilework, then collaging three direct quotes taken from the poem to sustain each side, and finally crafting a picturesque watercolor on the interior to represent the fortification of enduring love and reverence a mother has for her children.

The Military and Combat

15. Taps

Poet:

It took me forty years to talk or write about the sexual assault and sexual harassment that happened to me at initial training in the military. I never spoke about it to anyone. I speak more about that in a poem called "Into the Light," featured later in this book. "Taps" speaks to the absolute dread that I experienced as my perpetrator's footsteps echoed loudly down the barracks hall coming towards me, and to how so many years later that sound can still terrify me. Christina outdid herself with the art for "Taps." What a brilliant idea to record herself reading the poem while she intensely attacked the canvas, exactly capturing the intensity of this poem. It also wasn't lost on me that she painted it horizontally, but displays it vertically, further demonstrating her versatility and the deep, darker meaning behind "Taps."

Artist:

"Taps" is a 15" x 30" mixed media collage created from black acrylic paint mixed with dry medium black flakes hex. Lisa once told me that this poem was about sound. That there were taps on the shoes her assaulter wore. That the sound of him coming down the hall, the tapping sound his shoes made, has been forever seared into her brain. Sounds. This was a unique poem about sounds, and how distinctive abhorrence to particular sounds can scar you for life.

I was at first perplexed at how to visually display this revulsion to a sound. Then I had the idea to do everything in real time: mix the paint, read the poem, paint the piece. The outcome is a video recording of me reading the poem while painting the piece in real time—the tapping of the brush, the scraping of the canvas, the urgency of the effect. The final piece is as dark as it is obscure, as bleak as it is disconsolate—but one thing it is not is quiet.

16. Snowflakes from Above

Poet:

This is a lighter poem that speaks of how a young officer can easily be intimidated by those very senior to her. I would frequently get these small white memos from the colonel or general I worked for and had to decipher their meaning. Since the memos were affectionately nicknamed snowflakes, I wrote "Snowflakes from Above" to represent the experience of being on the receiving end of many a snowflake. Looking back now, it is just comical how I reacted. But at the time, as a young officer, I was working very hard and taking my professional role seriously. I think the colonels and generals wrote some of them just to mess with me and remind me who was in charge. There was no need for that. I clearly knew I wasn't.

Artist:

"Snowflakes from Above" is an 8" x 10" mixed media watercolor collage. I created this piece by making a pencil sketch and watercolor painting of the cubicles the junior officers used to sit in (pretty standard) then collaging the "Snowflakes from Above" a.k.a. our memos from the colonels and generals and other "good idea fairies" that had us doing their bidding. Lisa has pretty much nailed the lingo in her poem here. I just tried to illustrate how it feels to get inundated with memos from the beyond—or mostly the above in these cases.

17. Ode to a White Dude

Poet:

"Ode to a White Dude" is all about thanking the very few (less than a handful) white officers and commanders I worked for. It is sort of like a letter just to them. I wanted them to know just how much of a difference they made in my professional development with their mentorship and sponsorship. Leadership brings responsibility to teach, guide and, well, lead others. I had both great and terrible leaders while I served my country. These handful were the best, as they practiced inclusionary leadership long before the term became a force multiplier towards achieving an organization's mission. I was able to grow and develop as a leader, reaching levels of success that I might not have been able to achieve without their courage in taking a chance on someone so different from themselves.

The art piece for this poem, almost like a comic character, was a great way to represent the white dudes I wrote about in the poem. They stood out to me after 30 years of service. We need more leaders like that, who are not afraid to lead everyone and not just some.

Artist:

"Ode to a White Dude" is an 8" x 10" traditional collage created from an assortment of acid-free papers. I created this illustration by making a traditional silhouette out of assorted papers and layering them on top of one another to create the shadowed effect. I chose the earth tone hues to represent the time period between Lisa's 2004 desert camo deployment and then through the digitalized DCU years as well—using natural and plant-based designs within the papers chosen as a nod to these white dude's differences as compared to their toxic counterparts.

18. Every Day Was Tuesday

Poet:

"Every day is Tuesday" was a common refrain in the combat environment at the base I was serving at as a commander in Iraq. I can still hear troops repeating this over and over again in my mind, and I wanted to reflect on it for this poem in a somewhat comical way. Humor was something that got many of us through the dark periods while in that adverse environment. Days can start to roll into each other, and you can lose all sense of time as your concentration is so focused on mission accomplishment. The almost blitzkrieg pace of the base buildup in the Sunni Triangle was due to the dedication and herculean efforts of so many who served and was the best way for me to track time. I appreciate how Christina used my pictures of the base buildup for the matting all around the words of the poem in her art piece.

Artist:

"Every Day Was Tuesday" is an 18" x 15" mixed media collage that began as a charcoal piece of mortars set against the moon (because that is the only thing that really doesn't change all that much in Mortaritaville—the night sky and ordnance raining down) with a worn acrylic skin of the poem as the centerpiece. Then I found this old frame at a church yard sale and Lisa sent me a bunch of photos from her time in Iraq on LSA Anaconda, and we once again had a great collaboration idea to surround the image I had already created with alternating pictures of her unit doing the everyday tasks that were so seemingly mundane and routine. Thus, I believe we were able to successfully illustrate the monotony of deployments, which are also nightly interspersed with rocket fire and the heart-wrenching fear of a combat AOR.

19. DALT

Poet:

"DALT" is about the bonds one can form with others in uniform, even more so while serving in a combat environment where every action can have life or death implications. I've mentored lots of young officers and noncommissioned officers, and gave many of them nicknames, but DALT is one I can never forget and continue to mentor to this day. This poem speaks to the depth of bonds forged forever under the hail of hundreds of rockets and mortars. These types of bonds that some military personnel form and maintain are hard to replicate outside of the military.

Artist:

"DALT" is an 8" x 10" mixed media watercolor collage made from various acid-free papers. We all probably can remember a "Dumb Assed Lieutenant" at one time or another. But for Lisa, this one was a term of endearment, her hand-picked "exec" during her deployment in Iraq, and that says a lot.

Originally we were just going to put a photograph of them together and I wasn't going to do a piece for this poem, but Lisa ended up asking me to do one when she found some photographs she thought would work. So I found some papers that were the color of the infamous "butter bar" of the 2LT rank and the silver of the 1LT represented in the rank of the bar I created in watercolor in the middle of the piece—the rank he served in with her in Iraq—his DALT rank that cemented their mentorship and relationship for the ages. The piece just came together after that—not too shabby for a DALT.

20. Christian in a Foxhole

Poet:

I am a woman of faith, having grown up in the church. "Christian in a Foxhole" was written to represent that faith and to share my thoughts when I landed in Iraq. I had no fear of dying as I landed in that combat location, as I knew I had the power of my Lord with me. In my gear was a small Bible that one of my primas had given me, and I treasured that along with a small American flag provided by the Boy Scouts. I had already reconciled in my mind that I might not make it out and, due to my faith, I was able to concentrate fully on the task at hand. It liberated me to lead fully and to be always present. That doesn't mean that at times I didn't get scared, because I did.

I like the way Christina captured the essence of this poem. The way she filled the chapel steeple, with the many pictures of rockets and mortars, was just perfect. We really did use the mortar pieces that hit our base as the hanging bells in that steeple.

Artist:

"Christian in a Foxhole" is a 9" x 12" mixed media watercolor collage. I created this collage with pictures of the Chapel tent they built up on Lisa's base in Iraq (equipped with mortar bell tower), watercolors, acid-free papers, medal circle charm, and a medal cross bead. I used several different collage techniques at the same time in this piece to give the chapel more depth—cutting out in some areas while adding on more paper in others. The shelter this building gave to Lisa during her deployment represents more than just accommodating her body—which was why it was important to create such an elaborate visual quality of depth when constructing the collage.

21. The Combat You

Poet:

I am two people: the one that was before combat and the one that remains post-combat. In "The Combat You" I wanted to convey just how intensely one can change after experiencing combat and encountering death frequently. It is deeply personal and describes the struggle that I have with PTSD, dealing with powerful memories and the reality of reconciling those experiences with daily life outside the combat environment. Christina created an amazing art piece to depict this poem. She absolutely nailed it! I think she was able to do that because she also served in combat and has also been forever changed, another way we connect. Combat changes you.

Artist:

"The Combat You" is an 11" x 14" acrylic painting. I took one of Lisa's command photos and reimagined it for this painting to exemplify how one is forever changed after experiencing combat. The photo is inverted (flag is on the wrong side, a signal of warning, all is not well, etc.) the colors are just a bit off, stars are missing from the flag, proportions of the body are slightly wrong, and most of all you can see the wear and strain in the face. It's like you can almost capture a look of how you once were, but you can never go back completely, no matter how much you scrub or try to repaint yourself to the way you think you once were.

22. Eye Fuckery

Poet:

I would venture to say that lots of people know exactly what I describe in this poem, but am not sure that as many truly understand just how devastating it can be to the person on the receiving end. "Eye Fuckery" was written to describe what that feels like. The poem is intense and vulgar on purpose because the action itself is. I could have selected from a variety of my past experiences with this issue, but purposely chose a situation that occurred while serving in combat to demonstrate just how vile and out of place this is. There is never a situation where "eye fuckery" should be tolerated, least of all in combat.

I knew that this poem would be hard to bring to life in an art piece, but Christina's talent is on full view for us to appreciate as we look at "Eye Fuckery." I hope both my poem and her art can inform more people about this. I liked how Christina put eyes in the back of some heads and gave at least one three eyes. Now, this is art!

Artist:

"Eye Fuckery" is an 8" x 10" mixed media collage fashioned out of doll eyes, several different varieties of eyeball stamps, magazine pictures, ink, and paper. "Just another hazard in the AOR," yes, but how do you get this across? How can you make the viewer as uncomfortable as a woman in a dining hall in Iraq or Afghanistan?

That was the challenge for me with this illustration, until I found a pack of 100 doll eyes on Amazon. You can do a lot with a hundred doll eyes. I also found a myriad of different eyeball stamps. Amazing selection. Once I dug through all my Army magazines to find the perfect base image, I could adjust accordingly with cutting and pasting of the poem's words and, of course, the doll eyes. This is when I find our collaboration to be the most meaningful—when you can convey a highly complex concept like "Eye Fuckery" with just one poem and one image, when perhaps you didn't have the language or vocabulary to understand it at all until just then. Men need to read this poem—and see this piece. All men, not just men in uniform. Let the un-comfortability commence!

23. Black Death

Poet:

I am angry and deeply saddened at the loss of life and the impact of the burn pits on so many of us who served. There are so many living with serious medical conditions because of exposure from the burn pits. In Iraq, I saw the black smoke 24/7; it never abated. I wrote "Black Death" to speak to the horrors of the burn pits' aftermath. We didn't know then, us boots on the ground, what the exposures were doing to us. Someone should have known and done something about it then, not after so many deaths and destruction to our bodies. We were fighting enemies on multiple fronts and didn't realize the deadliest enemy was already inside our gates, silently killing us. Christina did a great job with the art for "Black Death." She and I are only two of the many who have been impacted by the burn pits' exposure, and my heart cries for the many we have already lost.

Artist:

"Black Death" is an 11" x 14" mixed media collage created from acid-free papers, plastic, and acrylic paint. Since many of my own illnesses have been attributed by the VA to burn pits, this poem rang very true to me. Thus, it was extremely important that I find a way to visually represent this topic in a manner that could not only enlighten viewers new to this subject matter but also approach this area with all the focus and attention it deserves. This piece is my attempt to broach an issue graphically, using words in tandem with images that concretely offer the viewer a way to comprehend our concern.

24. Echoes of War

Poet:

This is the only poem in the collection that I co-wrote with a fellow woman combat veteran, Sue Caldwell, and I am grateful to her for agreeing that I should include it. "Echoes of War" describes graphically our experiences in each of the wars where we served, Vietnam and Iraq. I have never bonded so quickly and deeply with another woman vet before; our personal lives and military and combat experiences were all too familiar. Although we had intense experiences in combat, we found that talking about it with each other helped lessen the burdens we carried. Sue was the first person with whom I could really share my darkest thoughts about my combat experiences.

I pray that all veterans who carry such heavy burdens have a "Sue" that can help them unpack their deepest, darkest thoughts of combat. I found out I was not alone in my thoughts, and that has made a huge difference in moving forward. Christina really got the words in this poem. Perhaps it resonated, as she is one of three generations of women who have served. I am very grateful to her for getting the intensity of the meaning behind "Echoes of War" and capturing the vivid colors on her canvas.

Artist:

"Echoes of War" is a 16" x 20" mixed media acrylic collage. When I spoke with Lisa about this piece before starting, she had an idea of doing something abstract. I liked that, because how can you describe war? I have two deployments myself (Kuwait/Iraq 2003 and Afghanistan 2008), and of all the lines in the poem, everything about bombs and rockets and things that kill and go boom, it is "Our bodies keep the score" that resonated over and over in my mind the most—and what ended up coming out on the canvas. I painted with palette knives instead of brushes, cutting into the canvas with primary colors to arrest the senses, and I left the echoes of this poem embedded within.

25. Cocktail

Poet:

This poem had not even been thought of or planned for this collection. However, when Christina told me that she always wanted to make a sculpture of all her pain medicine bottles, I knew I had to write "Cocktail" and informed her that she could indeed make that sculpture. This was another example of the great collaboration between us. This poem is so personal to me, and that is why maybe I hadn't considered it before. It speaks to while I was still on active duty, in my final years, and sought out mental health help. I went against all I had been taught, to never show weakness and seek assistance. As a commander, I just sucked it up and marched on, but had reached the limits of my physical body. "Cocktail" tells that journey of seeking help and what happened.

Artist:

"Cocktail" is a 19" x 12" mixed media sculpture made out of my VA prescription pill bottles and paper. I first came up with this basic idea when I read Lisa's other poem "Pain." We scrapped that one because the idea didn't fit, but then Lisa wrote the words for "Cocktail." I definitely think the words cascading out of the pill bottles fit this nicely. Another great collaboration.

26. Command

Poet:

I've always wanted to be a leader and was really drawn to leadership. In the military, my dream was to command at multiple levels. "Command" describes the nuance of military command and the heavy responsibility that one carries as a commander. It was my honor and privilege to serve as a commander in the military. This was where my leadership was acutely honed and set the stage for me to lead as a civilian and entrepreneur. Christina had a great idea to use the outline of my eagle rank as the backdrop for the art piece for "Command." I also commanded at levels below colonel, but this piece depicts leadership at my most senior level in both peacetime and combat. The eagles were on full view in this piece inside both the outline and within.

Artist:

"Command" is an 8" x 10" mixed media collage created with acid-free papers and semi-gloss acrylic medium. Lisa had the honor and privilege to serve as a commander both in CONUS and while in combat in Iraq. She was able to send me pictures from these commands for this piece, so that I could feature in the illustration how being a commander is not only one of the toughest, but also one of the most rewarding jobs in all of the military. Hopefully I was able to convey this idea by allowing you to catch a glimpse of her commands through the highest rank she achieved, Colonel.

27. Latina Warrior

Poet:

When I first went into the military, I downplayed my gender and my ethnicity. I was trying hard to assimilate and be like the white pilot leaders that I had. It took a few years for me to realize that my gender and ethnicity are what gave me precious insight into others. They are like force multipliers, enabling me to be the best leader that I could be.

"Latina Warrior" was written in both English and Spanish to honor my culture, my gender, and the leader warrior that I am. Parts of me were muted during my service, and I felt that I could never be truly authentic. However, each and every day I dug deep and relied on both my heritage and my lived experiences to lead with empathy and distinction. I really was the "Latina Warrior" as I led in peacetime, combat, and higher education, and now as an entrepreneur.

Wow, Christina did a fabulous piece of art for this signature poem! I absolutely love the level of detail inside; it is quite busy but captures all the aspects of Latina and Warrior and the juxtaposition of the two. You must really look at this piece to get all that it has to offer. Every time I look at it, I find something that I missed. This was the last poem I wrote for the collection, and it was the last art piece that Christina completed. What a great way to sum up our powerful collaboration. I know that this will not be our final collaborative effort. There is much more in our future.

Artist:

"Latina Warrior" is a 36" x 24" truly mixed media collage made up of the author's own medals, decorations, ranks, uniforms, Always Javelinas tote, bookmarks, handout cards, photographs, papers, handmade tablecloth, handcrafted wallets, Iraqi currency, unit patches, handmade Mexican coasters, assorted stickers, Texas A&M University-Kingsville bag, and University of Texas at San Antonio sticker, plus an assortment of acid-free papers. Created over a period of more than a month, this collage was delicately and thoughtfully pieced together using a photograph from the author's Iraq deployment as a guide.

As with our 49 other collaborations, the communication back and forth with "Latina Warrior" was the perfect amount of thoroughness mixed with cooperation. Whenever there was a request for information or input, the other partner stepped up immediately with a response. I'm extremely proud to call this our finale piece and cannot wait to collaborate on our next project!

Life After the Military

28. Transition Blisters

Poet:

Most veterans experience some issues with transitioning into the civilian workforce after serving. I was no different. It doesn't really matter what rank you are, there will be some type of issues for everyone. For me it wasn't about the job or role I would undertake, it was about the psychological transition and loss of identity that I experienced initially.

"Transition Blisters" was written to touch on my experiences with that, but also to highlight the lighter side of transition, like what to wear each day. That to me was the most painful part of my transition. No job intimidated me, but having to figure out different clothes to wear each day wore me down. You laugh; I'm serious. I would stand in front of my closet for hours each day to decide what to wear and what accessories would work for an outfit. I still miss my combat boots.

Artist:

"Transition Blisters" is a 9" x 12" mixed media watercolor collage. Simple pen and ink sketch with watercolor painting inspired by the final words of the poem: "Finally figured out the whole accessorizing thing!" Lisa had a lot of ideas, many having to do with mirrors, and looking into them, one with a uniform, one in civilian clothes. But we settled on this little ditty because I really liked the simplicity, and I liked how the lines of the poem could match up with the transition of the pants at the knees as well. The image is also stepping into her future, as she finally figured out the whole accessorizing thing. So I appreciate the depth that it all gives here.

29. Invisible Veteran

Poet:

This poem had been swimming inside my head for quite some time. Thoughts of it came to me every time I had to go to a Veterans Affairs appointment in person, or when I was at an event that focused on veterans. I just felt that at times I was invisible, as a woman who had served her country. That no one really saw me or acknowledged my contribution. Many times, I would look around at the physical surroundings that I was in and only see pictures of white men in uniform looking back at me. My invisibility was even more pronounced as I am a woman of color, a Latina. Never quite fitting in with what most consider to be the image of a veteran or a combat veteran.

"Invisible Veteran" captures how I really feel as a woman veteran, among a culture and community that still diminishes my service. I was honored to have "Invisible Veteran" be part of the unveiling of the VA's new, more inclusive mission statement in early 2023. I love that Christina immediately saw herself in this poem. It truly resonated with her, and she used herself in the art as the "Invisible Veteran." As a poet, I cannot be more honored when my art resonates with others, especially when they can see themselves in my words.

Artist:

"Invisible Veteran" is a 48" x 30" mixed media acrylic collage and one of the very first collaborations that Lisa and I did together, before "Latina Warrior." My process was taking a picture from my Afghanistan deployment with the CJTF-101 in 2008 and painting a very quick palette knife self-portrait—leaving the face blank. I then scribbled the lines of the poem, like bathroom stall graffiti, behind the figure, like white noise in the background of the portrait—to argue with the viewer, leaving the final line, the refrain of the whole poem on the face…do you see me? The almost-life-size-ness of the portrait challenges the viewer with the final question that one can no longer avoid: Is it deliberate or ignorance?

30. Superwoman Is Dead

Poet:

I've spoken previously about the pursuit of perfection in our lives, especially for women and above all women of color, using the title of this poem to make my point. "Superwoman Is Dead" describes my journey to achieve perfection in all aspects of my life and the reality that it is simply unachievable. I learned this the hard way and can attest to the fact that it is okay to put work first one day, your family the other, as circumstances dictate. The hard part is knowing which one is the priority on a given day. Once I allowed myself to not be perfect, I became a better mother, friend, colleague, and leader. The effort I put into the pursuit of perfection, I could put into actually being and living.

Artist:

"Superwoman Is Dead" is an 11" x 14" pen and ink watercolor collage with acrylic skins that hit me extremely close to home. When I read this poem, I knew exactly what I was going to sketch and whose grave the flowers were going to cover: my own.

The beauty of crafting a watercolor pen and ink collage is all about time: having to skillfully wait for different mediums to dry and how to then manipulate just the right amount of water for each tint and hue to dry. It also takes time to construct the acrylic skins to put the words of the poem onto the grave, which in turn had to be on an already dried surface. These were all choices made, to make a skin versus just cutting and pasting paper to the piece—but I made the choice to have the words be transparent to the grave, giving them an ethereal look, an aged look as well, so as you visit this grave to this superwoman who is dead, to this woman and her unattainable goals, you may read the words or you may no longer be able to, as they disappear with wear and time.

31. Save the Civilians

Poet:

"Save the Civilians" describes a PTSD flashback that I experienced in an airport parking garage. It tells of the stark realities of the invisible wounds of combat that can linger long after one walks off the battlefield and comes home. I wanted to convey the fear and bewilderment that I had when I experienced it and the trepidation of wondering when and where I might experience that level of intense flashback again. "Save the Civilians" provides a peek into the mind of one suffering from PTSD and combat-related trauma.

Artist:

"Save the Civilians" is a 9" x 12" mixed media watercolor collage inspired by the idea that you can be two people at once when you are in the middle of a PTSD episode. Note the two large images of Lisa, both in a "command" mode pose, centered in a regular everyday airport terminal. I am conveying the idea of ordinariness here. That anyone could have a PTSD trigger happen from an ordinary sound, a natural smell, or even an intrusive thought and then BOOM (like the colorful star shapes signify here) you can be right back in the thick of it! Or, as it suggests in the blurred image of Lisa, something that she carries with her all the time. She is always in the thick of it, because she carries PTSD with her wherever she goes.

32. The Sisterhood

Poet:

This was an extremely easy poem for me to write, I had just left Washington, DC, where I participated in an event at the Military Women's Memorial that honored and recognized women veterans. I was grateful to be awarded a handmade quilt from Quilts of Honor and to participate in an art exhibit hosted by Uniting US that included two of my poems. To say I was deeply affected would be an understatement. "The Sisterhood" began as a seed on my return flight and, once I arrived home, I crafted it with the names of the organizations that hosted the events in the phrasing as a way to show my gratitude.

The art piece for this poem is outstanding. I love Christina's creativity and ability to express what I've written. The art absolutely captures the essence of "The Sisterhood." What makes this collaboration so very special is that the piece includes beautiful memories of our time together in fellowship with women veterans at various Uniting US events.

Artist:

"The Sisterhood" is a 24" x 24" mixed media acrylic collage. I immediately identified with this poem because I first met Lisa at a Uniting US event at the Military Women's Memorial when my grandmother, my mom and I received a quilt from the Quilts of Honor! I just name dropped all three organizations from her poem in that one sentence:) which gave me the idea for the piece because I had a quilt AND pictures from that event and several other UnitingUS.org events that I have attended since then with Lisa and many other amazing women veterans that have widened our powerful sisterhood to this day. To honor them, I hand crafted a paper collage quilt with glitter stiches, wrapped around two delicately pieced-together women under an intricately acrylic painted aquamarine sky.

33. You Get Me

Poet:

After I witnessed on national TV the cluster of a withdrawal of United States troops from Afghanistan, I was deeply affected by the way it occurred. Memories of leaving Vietnam flashed in my mind. I knew right then that many of my fellow veterans would begin to question what we did in Afghanistan and Iraq. Many would begin to question their own service and contributions. I wanted them to know that we serve for a variety of reasons, but especially for each other. When engaging with other veterans, invariably I would think to myself that they really do get me. We have so many shared experiences that many civilians have a hard time understanding. "You Get Me" was written as a message to my fellow veterans, to affirm their service and sacrifice. The art for "You Get Me" is another great example of Christina's creativity and how she does really get me.

Artist:

"You Get Me" is a 9"x 12" mixed media collage that pays homage to everyone who has been "there." I liked how Lisa used the refrain "You get me" over and over in this poem as emphasis, so I used those words as a graphic starting point for this illustration. Text can be elegant and pleasing to the eye when used in artwork; however, I wanted it to be a bit rough around the edges here because we are talking about imperfect beings—and how you get me in all my flaws, right? The viewer gets a glimpse into our world here; a brief little look into what we have accomplished, what we have endured, and what we have yet to attempt through these letters—like windows into our souls. You get me?

34. Get Out of My Head

Poet:

Like many veterans, I suffer from tinnitus. Mine is severe, and there are days when it is almost unbearable. "Get Out of My Head" expresses the desperation I sometimes feel when it rages. I am embarrassed to admit that I would walk around my house screaming, "Get out of my head!" until I realized that it wasn't coming from an external source. Okay, I further admit that I still sometimes yell around my house for the noise to get out of my head. It is super annoying and loud. It affects me negatively in more ways than I care to admit.

Artist:

"Get Out of My Head" is a 12" x 12" mixed media collage created with paper, acrylic skins, acrylic dry medium (mica flakes and ground marble) and acrylic satin gel medium. Any veteran who worked on a flight light or in a convoy, or was around any light to heavy machinery, can relate to this poem.

However, my goal with this particular piece was to have Lisa visually represent the experience of all *female* veterans (note the acrylic skins that are 'within' her head—they are images taken from recent Army and veteran magazine publications) not only what it is like to feel an annoying sound in your head, but then again to be exploited by the same system you go to for help, our own medical organizations where we have to all but demand to be seen for combat/deployment-related illnesses and injuries. So not only do you have this nonstop sound in your head, but once you get through "the system" you are so poked, pinched, and prodded you are no longer recognizable to yourself. And that is IF they believe you that you are hearing anything in the first place.

35. VetSpeak

Poet:

Veterans have their own culture, and with that comes their own type of language. Writing "VetSpeak" was an amusing way of sharing a bit of insight into that language. I also wanted to share that the use of profanity sometimes just means nothing, a place holder or space filler. I must state clearly that not all veterans or military personnel use profanity or vulgar language. Just so happens that the ones I've been around lately do, myself included.

Christina's first version of the art for this poem entailed using the word fuck multiple times, 18 actually. I counted. Soooo, I went back to her and, ahem, explained why I thought we could use other words and acronyms and minimize the number of fucks. After some back and forth, I was super grateful that she acquiesced.

Artist:

"Vet Speak" is an 8" x 10" mixed media collage created out of acrylic paint pens and wooden tiles. "Fuck was just a comma" was the last line of this poem and also the line that inspired my idea for this piece—it had no inherent meaning, no attack, no extravagant or vicious denotation. It was just a common pause, a filler, a gap. I originally had the idea of just a whole Scrabble board filled up with the word. But I think Lisa shot me down. I still like the idea, still think it goes with her broader meaning of the majority of this poem, that concentrates on the one word—but this works too. Vets do speak a lot in acronyms still. It's just ingrained in us. But I don't think using acronyms was the gist of this poem, you know? I mean, WTF?

36. Death of a Wife

Poet:

This and the poem that follows are the only two in this collection that I wrote in the third person. I found that to be more comfortable for me, and perhaps some people will be better able to relate to them since I did so. "Death of a Wife" is indeed about my role as a wife and the finality of that existence. I had to experience the death of the role almost like the death of an individual, in order for me to truly feel the rebirth. I was glad that Christina really resonated with this poem and liked how she was able to create art to represent the sentiments behind it.

Artist:

"Death of a Wife" is an 8"x 10" mixed media watercolor collage mounted with a 3.5" matte in a 15"x 19" frame. I fell in love with this poem as soon as I read it, because I could relate as a twice-divorced person myself, so I took illustrating it to heart, with a bit of fun on the side. I found a frame one would use as a guestbook or for well wishes at a reception and repurposed it for snippets of the poem (written like it would be if you were leaving your remarks for the happy couple). Then I designed what, in my mind's eye, would be the world's perfect divorcee gown, what one would wear when one "stoically attended the wake" before going out to "totally rock the celebration of life," which of course would include a bouquet of flowers that I created featuring jewelry from vintage Tiffany & Co catalogs.

37. Death of a Marriage

Poet:

This is the second poem in the collection written in the third person. "Death of A Marriage" is a companion piece to "Death of a Wife" and describes my thoughts on my own marriage. After a lengthy marriage, I divorced. With reflection, I realized that the marriage had expired years before it breathed its final breath. Since its death, I have been free to enjoy friends and family, to completely experience my faith, to unleash my creative side, and to live fully in the light. Christina and I discussed the best way to capture this poem. I had the idea to somehow use skeletons. She absolutely took that simple idea and created a unique way to depict the poem.

Artist:

"Death of a Marriage" is a 9" x 12" mixed media watercolor collage. I began this piece with a simple pen and ink drawing of a married couple, albeit skeletonized, who have seen better days, as you can see by their body language in relation to each other. The shine is off these marital clothes, which is why the watercolor hues chosen were all subdued forms of white, creams, blacks, and greys. And unlike in the "Death of a Wife" piece, which is celebratory in its blackish tints, there are no bridal bouquets here to hand out, only smoldering cigarettes that are fuming close to the bone. There are some heirloom pieces of jewelry from a vintage Tiffany & Co catalog barely hanging on to the skeletal bride, but who knows for how much longer, as this marriage ceases to exist right before our eyes.

38. Not an Imposter

Poet:

I know I am not the only one that occasionally deals with imposter syndrome. I exude a confidence unmatched by some, so how can it be that I also experience doubt in whatever roles I take on? "Not an Imposter" shares that despite reaching success across multiple areas, I still at times feel like an imposter. I know better. And so should you. Let's keep reminding ourselves that we deserve to be where we are at, and that we are indeed worthy.

Artist:

"Not an Imposter" is a 9" x 12" mixed media watercolor pen and ink collage. I started this piece by intricately painting a small watercolor version of Lisa in her "command" pose. I then applied a very thin layer of water, just on top of the portrait. I immediately wiped subtly away at the image, leaving a faint trail of watercolor tint behind the image. Finally, I penned in the most apropos lines of the poem below the newly captured figure to express the feelings of this latest likeness.

39. Mi Pastora

Poet:

I am so pleased to be able to honor my pastor with this poem. My faith and pastor are important aspects of my life. Pastor Lupina is an amazing selfless woman, as I describe in "Mi Pastora." Her spiritual leadership continues to add much to my life, and I am so very grateful the Lord put her in my path. I knew that I wanted a Methodist cross to be a focal part of the art for this poem. I so like how Christina did this piece, and the way she was able to depict my pastor in action.

Artist:

"Mi Pastora" is a 9" x 12" mixed media collage made with several different acid-free papers, gold foil paper, pictures, watercolor, and semi-gloss acrylic medium. Inspired by Lisa's amazing Mexican Methodist pastor, this piece is a little window into her and her church's soul—courtesy of some wonderful pictures Lisa emailed to me. Using some gold foil papers, as well as watercolor paper and watercolors, I recreated the Methodist cross as a window into Lisa's pastora. I used the semi-gloss acrylic medium as a topcoat for the pictures, as well as to give them a painterly finish.

Healing and the Road to Authenticity

40. Into the Light

Poet:

"Into the Light" deals with the harsh realities of finally being able to speak up about having been sexually assaulted at initial training, after many years of silence. Since it was during the pandemic, I decided to use the coronavirus as an analogy to educate the public. This poem also discusses how the horrific murder of Vanessa Guillén became the catalyst for me to find my voice and to speak up. This was the first poem I ever wrote, and it was written from a place of pain and shame for what happened to me and for not speaking up sooner.

Artist:

"Into the Light" was the first poem I received from Lisa, launching our collaboration. In hindsight, it established the creative precedent of how we ended up working together over the next year. It was essential for us to understand how to communicate our ideas, in order to get them across visually in a way that was satisfying to both artist and author. For example, I would begin by asking Lisa to give me an idea of where her head was while writing the poem (here she felt tethered down, like her legs were roots at the beginning of the poem). Next, I re-imagine her poetry into a 9" x 12" mixed media watercolor collage – not only breaking through into the light, but bringing the light forth with her because she is such an inspiration to me and other women, military members, and survivors. This successful collaboration on "Into the Light" is a great example of the healing power of art and the sisterhood of veterans that can last a lifetime.

41. MST Warrior

Poet:

"MST Warrior" describes my journey with military sexual trauma (MST) and how after writing my own MST story, along with 13 others, in my book *Stories from the Front: Pain, Betrayal, and Resilience on the MST Battlefield*, I am now able to speak up and advocate for change and let others know they are not alone. In this poem, I own my trauma and begin to move away from being a victim and a survivor to becoming a warrior who takes a stand to help herself and others. I was awed by the art for this poem. Christina got the whole moving past being a victim and a survivor to something much more, the warrior.

Artist:

"MST Warrior" is a 9"x 12" mixed media collage that incorporates real dried flowers, semi-precious obsidian gemstones, and acrylic gel skins. I figured that a poem that has in its beginning few lines, "Never a victim, much more than a survivor" deserves a piece that is also much more than just art—the obsidian gemstone used to create the hair is commonly referred to as a stone for warriors, known for protection and strong healing energies. The jacket is created from an intricate mixed media process of acrylic gel skins, which bolsters it in an armor-like appearance, using the powerful words of the poem for its fortification. And finally, Lisa sits upon a "commanding tsunami" of real dried flowers, representing the empowered MST Warriors she now leads to justice. Together it is wrapped in a custom cherry wood frame hand crafted by my father, Rich Helferich, symbolizing good fortune, happiness, and strength.

42. The Grunt and the Colonel

Poet:

I interviewed many individuals for my first book about military sexual trauma, *Stories from the Front: Pain, Betrayal, and Resilience on the MST Battlefield*. This poem is about the grunt I interviewed who had served in Vietnam. Our journeys, both personally and professionally, had so many parallels that I felt compelled to write "The Grunt and the Colonel" after our interviews. I am humbled to call the grunt my friend and kindred spirit. Christina did a terrific job on the art for this poem. The varying ways she was able to depict both the colonel and the grunt are really creative and special.

Artist:

"The Grunt and the Colonel" is an 11" x 14" mixed media collage that is near and dear to my heart, because it is all about multigenerational women in the military and how we relate to one another. The poem addresses how Lisa (the Colonel) and her friend (the Grunt) cross generational barriers by talking about PTSD from their respective deployments and military assignments. I visually represent how they overlap in time and space by placing them together on the canvas, with silhouettes combining to form one shape—their camouflage color palettes representing their particular war (jungle vs desert). I replaced the typical camo pattern with beautiful foliage, butterflies, stars, suns, moons, and crystals to exemplify and honor their femininity—something that was often mocked and held against them. And because my mom is also a Vietnam-era veteran (Diane Helferich – Army Nurse Corps 1969-1971), I immediately identified with this poem; therefore, I knew I needed to make this piece as beautiful as she is so we can, as the last line suggests, continue to help each other heal.

43. La Rona/The Trickster

Poet:

Covid certainly had an impact on me. It was such a trickster of a virus, with varying symptoms starting and stopping. I wrote "La Rona/The Trickster" on Christmas Day, at the lowest and most desperate point of my illness. I missed my family and friends so very much but was grateful to be alive. What better way for a writer, a poet, to capture the conflicting emotions and feelings of an illness than to write a poem to share with others. Several of my friends had Covid when I did, so we shared our experiences, and this poem is the result of my experience and theirs.

I really like how Christina used her own image to reflect herself as the one with Covid. She saw herself under the influence of "La Rona/The Trickster". Unfortunately, am sure that many more will be able to do the same.

Artist:

"La Rona, The Trickster" is a 9" x 12" pen and ink watercolor illustrating how I imagined La Rona looked playing around inside our bodies after Lisa put a name to her in this poem. I thought about her juggling the virus around in one lung then skipping on over to the next, all the while laughing and messing around with her cousin jesters and auntie clowns—until their whole network of fools has thoroughly invaded every organ of our bodies—and then their Covid joke they are carrying is on us.

44. Fractured

Poet:

This poem captures the intensely personal thoughts and feelings I have as I reflect on my sexual assault at initial training in the military. I don't think I could have written "Fractured" if I hadn't undergone therapy with the VA. In fact, the poem actually helped me move a bit further down the road in my healing journey. It allowed me the ability to look back and acknowledge that it is okay to remember only the parts that I can and be okay to not know the entirety.

The art for this poem is one of my favorites in the collection. It truly captures the fractured shards of memory regarding my sexual assault and the way sometimes I do feel like a specimen under observation or analysis. Christina's art is an outstanding visual interpretation of "Fractured."

Artist:

"Fractured" is a 14" x 12" mixed media collage that I constructed inside of a shadowbox out of straight pins, paper, fabric, and plastic gemstones, to recreate the idea of an insect specimen box. Here we find the fractured mind of Lisa Carrington Firmin. Let us study her as we take her apart, piece by piece. Let us study how being fractured keeps her whole. Piece. By. Piece.

45. The Abyss

Poet:

I wrote "The Abyss" to describe what I was going through as I interviewed individuals that had experienced military sexual trauma. I found myself taking on their trauma, absorbing it as my own, and it nearly broke me. I was grateful that I was undergoing EMDR therapy at the time, as my therapist was able to provide me with tools to ensure I set and followed boundaries to keep the trauma of others from taking me down. It was an extremely difficult task for me, and I sometimes find myself in the abyss over and over again. What is important is that I know I can escape it. It is just so very hard at times.

Christina got the meaning behind "The Abyss" right away, and her art piece demonstrates the way one can get sucked into the swirl that leads down into "The Abyss." I really like the center; that's exactly what my words described. This was an early collaboration that encapsulated both our ideas perfectly.

Artist:

"The Abyss" is a 48" x 30" mixed media collage created with fabric, acrylic medium, acrylic paint, and acid-free paper and is one of the two first collaborations that Lisa and I did in 2021, before we started *Latina Warrior*. This almost life-size work demands that the viewer confront its center, drawing you near, round and round, down and down into its core. Some may spend a few glances, others drawn in for lengthier periods, but all are drawn to "The Abyss."

This was the sense I also got when I first read the poem and hence decided this could be one of our first collaborations, because I immediately had the idea of illustrating this in a very large, arresting way—to circle her poem around itself, almost dizzyingly so—in a way that the reader could feel the poem at the same time they were viewing it. Lisa came up with the idea to make the void in the center darker and murkier—something more sinister, to get lost in. This is the final result of both our ideas, bounced off each other, feedback heard and returned, teamwork!

46. The Breakup

Poet:

This poem speaks to the immensely tight bond that can form between a patient and their therapist, albeit more one-sided. When my EMDR therapist told me she was moving on to another role, I was stunned. Sat there with a mask hiding my true feelings. I wished her well, as the new role was more accommodating to her life. The next week I shared that I really wasn't okay and had written "The Breakup" so that I could help her understand just how much she meant to me and how much I was going to miss her. I truly felt like she was abandoning me. I am just grateful that her departure coincided with a milestone in my treatment and that I had the tools to move on.

    I laughed when Christina told me that she was almost done reading the poem and had already decided on how she was going to do the art, then got the shock that it wasn't a partner that I was describing, but my therapist. I wrote it that way on purpose. I wanted people to think about those in their life that had abandoned them and waited until the last stanza to admit who I was referring to.

Artist:

"The Breakup" is a 9"x 12" mixed media collage created with pen/ink and charcoal. I really enjoyed making this piece because it was like I was writing on the walls or something—some sort of illicit form of acting out over a breakup, right? That's what I was feeling when I first read Lisa's poem: those feelings coursing through me, about being abandoned or dejected. Then I got to those last few lines about the therapist, and I think I might have actually laughed out loud—AT MYSELF! I got sucked in thinking of myself, and I wasn't thinking of all the *other* ways I could have read the poem. That's when I got out my pens and charcoal and got to work on this piece—writing on all *my* emotional walls and leaving an empty chair for the therapist who just broke up with *me*.

47. Pain

Poet:

This was a difficult poem to write. I live with both physical and emotional pain, and there are times when it is hard to go on. In "Pain" I freely admit some of my darkest thoughts. My pain can be all consuming and lead to some very negative thoughts. I continue to try to find ways to deal with it, but that in itself can be extremely difficult. Am still working through the fact that I think I deserve pain. Writing "Pain" helped me get some of those dark thoughts out on paper, so I could unpack them one at a time. There is a lot to unpack.

This particular collaboration was one that we had lots of back and forth on. I wanted the art to portray the reality of intense pain and the darkness that can accompany it. I think the final piece does exactly that. This is not a lighthearted poem; it is meant to convey the desolation and isolation of pain.

Artist:

"Pain" is an 11" x 14" mixed media collage created from plastic, fabric, wax, paper, my VA pill bottles, pieces of my Army uniform, and a custom-made shadowbox frame by my father.

This was an interesting collaboration to create with Lisa. It started out as a sculpture of pill bottles, but Lisa decided this was not exactly the direction she wanted the poem to go—focused entirely on pills—and I completely saw her point. So I reread the poem and got my heat gun out and melted some pill bottles, and she liked that direction and asked, "Can you melt some bones too?" Of course I could! Now we were flowing in the same creative direction, so I melted some red wax and ripped up some of my old uniform pants I had left over from my Afghanistan deployment and began to scribble the poem on them—so they could hang off the canvas to add to that aesthetic—and then all we needed was my dad to hand craft a shadowbox to tie it all together. Lisa's continual feedback on this piece was integral to my process and shows how wonderfully collaboration can truly work in the healing power of art.

48. Wounded Not Worthless

Poet:

I wrote "Wounded Not Worthless" to pay tribute to my artist collaborator Christina, who has a company under the same name as the title of this poem. It seemed as if I had found another woman combat veteran with experiences similar to mine. Her personal and professional lives were all too close to my own.

I will not reveal who I was referring to as the "you" in the poem; I leave that up to your interpretation. Suffice it to say that after I wrote "Wounded Not Worthless" I realized that it was not only Christina's story I had described, but my own as well. Sadly, it is an all too familiar story for many others. Writing this was very therapeutic for me, and I believe it totally resonated and did the same for Christina. Our shared trauma came out in this poem and art piece. We both were in attack mode. Sometimes you just have to beat trauma into submission. We both got a huge jolt of further healing with this one. The final art piece is as intense as our experiences have been. Keeping it real, folks.

Artist:

"Wounded Not Worthless" is a 36"x 24" mixed media collage created with spray paint, acrylic paint, and paper that Lisa said was inspired by me (was it because my website is WoundedNotWorthless.com or that the first words of the poem are "Fuck you!"? lol)

Nonetheless, I must say, out of all the original pieces of art I created for this anthology, this one took me the longest to conceive. But once I had the concept, it not only came together quickly, it was also extremely healing and liberating. I took a combination of things from my life and items from the poem to get a true mixture of ideas, to bury old wounds directly into the canvas as well as declare life-affirming expressions on top of that debris. The absolute most important concept is that I was able to bury "You are an absolute stain on female veterans" with "Fuck You," "Victorious," "Reborn," and especially "Not Worthless"!

49. Life

Poet:

This very short poem illustrates the seasons of my life: my earlier tough road, the healing journey, and the ability to really live authentically. "Life" is a great example of how a poem doesn't have to be long or wordy to tell a story. In its very simple terms, it describes a long journey to find oneself. Christina was innovative with the materials and design she created for this poem. It is a great representation of my intention with "Life."

Artist:

"Life" is a 15" x 10.5" mixed media collage created with real dried flowers, metal clock parts, pen and ink on handmade paper. Lisa sent me this poem with the caption, "shortest poem ever!" We then talked about how in so few words she was able to convey the seasons of her life: pain, reflection, discovery, and learning to laugh and live more freely.

I thought to myself later, How can I visually do all that justice, when she summed it up so immaculately verbally?? Then I thought about time, and the words she used, like linger and languish. That's where I came up with using the handmade paper. It takes time to make paper, you have to linger over it, languish over it. And then what could signify listening, learning, and leading? Clock parts! Because we are all wound up so tight, we must unwind, wind, and do the winding at different times in our lives, right? And of course, flowers symbolize all the times we laugh and live and love. Combined all together? "Life".

50. Writing Is My Salvation

Poet:

I have found my voice as a storyteller. I am no longer allowing others to tell or write my story; I can now do that. I want to write stories that are not widely shared, those of underrepresented individuals or groups. I am controlling my own narrative. And it has made all the difference in living life to its fullest. "Writing Is My Salvation" is just that; writing saved my life and helped bring me out of the darkness into the light. Writing and documenting my journey is not only good to capture historical perspective for my experiences, but it inspires and gives life to others. We are meant to be the masters of our own destinies; writing allows me to do exactly that.

I appreciate the humor in the art for this poem. Although it is a serious poem, it shows the versatility in Christina's art. How we express ourselves can be interpreted in so many ways; it truly is in the eye of the beholder.

Artist:

"Writing Is My Salvation" is a 9" by 12" mixed media collage created with various acid-free papers, pen and ink. Two of the things I truly have in common with my collaborator are list making and doodling! We are birds of a feather when it comes to these little details, which is probably why we get along so well. So when I read this poem, I immediately saw her sitting at her writing desk, making lists and doodling on an errant sheet of paper, making sure she was hitting all the high points in her poetry. This was my fun (and cute) way of illustrating our creative process.

Afterword

As a fellow author and storyteller, I share Lisa Carrington Firmin's passion for drawing on faith, community, and strengths for healing from woundedness, expressing moral pain and facing moral injury. For many years, I have been called to do trauma-informed work with broken families, wounded, betrayed children, women with shattered trust, and now, veterans with hidden, invisible wounds. The secret wounds of military service are not well known or understood, and it is writers like Colonel Carrington Firmin who make the hidden visible and give voice to the unfathomable pain of betrayal and service-related trauma. This author instills faith and hope that, in the midst of horrible circumstances, we find new purpose and meaning in the ashes of our past. And, although what was lost can never be the same, the pain does not win.

This poetry and artwork – much of which is intriguing, visually stimulating multimedia – stand side by side in portraying the poet's life journey. They are clearly depicted and described by the poet and artist, but each reader will take his or her own truth from the pages. This collection is healing, as it does not leave the reader in despair, but rather embodies the process of pushing through the pain and putting the pieces back together with nurture, self-growth, and creativity, so that the new, self-evolving creation becomes a work of art. Colonel Carrington Firmin is like a skilled glassmaker, who subjects her shattered, cracked pieces to the heat and emerges as a new, complex, multi-dimensional creation. The journey depicted in *Latina Warrior* is one of a more-than-survivor self that strives for healing by sharing and reaching out to a community of others.

"*Latina Warrior* is my story," says Colonel Carrington Firmin. Actually, this exquisite volume of poetry and art is more than a story. A story is most often a left-brain logical narrative depiction or representation. This collection, a work of art, with imagery, metaphor, and trance-inducing language capable of sliding the reader back in time, is the person of Colonel Carrington Firmin, the very core of who she is across her lifespan, her life lived.

The early parts of the book speak transparently to her Latina background in a strong family with love, sibling competition, genuine relationships, and faith. Her lighthearted portrayal of childhood was one of cocky confidence and Latino roots of nurture, encouragement, intellectual growth, first-generation success, and challenge. Later in the book the emotional tone changes, and a darkness seeps into the writing. She is faced with the challenges of trying to succeed and survive in a male-dominated misanthropic world, one that shattered innocence and brought undeserved imposter syndrome, along with moral pain and places of stuck darkness. Colonel Carrington Firmin's courage to push through the pain arises out of these ashes. She seeks help and connects with others to face the pain and pursue healing and recovery. She sifts through the ashes, letting some things go, such as her marriage, yet drawing close to her faith and her sisterhood as a warrior and strong woman.

Latina Warrior is her journey lived, her persona, and it will speak to others as an archetypal representation of metamorphosis, moving from untouched childhood innocence to unexpected woundedness to the lost innocence of combat, to the quest for healing, recovery, and restoration. It is a collection to be slowly digested, returned to for sustenance, and kept by the bedside table for the nights that haunt and interrupt sleep. It will resonate with other female warriors who have lost their voice or not yet found words to depict what they have experienced and what they are seeking or yearning for. It will speak to other Latina women who are journeying from woundedness, to survivor, to one who conquers and thrives.

The military trains its members well to live in the space of left-brain logic, rational planning, and mission execution. It is not a place of art or poetry, and it discourages its members from feeling too deeply or processing emotional pain. Indeed, sometimes the system denies the presence of emotional pain. It can leave its members unable to emotionally process what has been experienced or labels the natural process of grief and loss as "weakness."

Poetry and art transcend time and place, residing in a right-brain pre-conscious, soul-searching place of metaphor, imagery, empathy, attachment, and intuition. Poetry and art are awakened by our deepest joys, losses, fears, shattered innocence, betrayed trust, and unexpected surges of pain or joy. Poetry and art capture and allow us to revisit sensory memories, strong emotions, taste, sounds, and sights, like the heat of the desert, the cries of children, the aftermath of devastation, and deep unexpected pain. It is like being back there again in an instant. Poetry and art also propel us toward healing, as the process itself stirs up new emotions and awareness in the midst of recognition of what can't be changed.

Colonel Carrington Firmin's poetry, perfectly paired with the compelling artwork of her fellow combat veteran Christina Helferich-Polosky, evokes a deeper understanding of self, and readers will experience a spontaneous "Yes!" and an "A-ha!" on absorbing the word pictures and visual imagery. These works not only depict Colonel Carrington Firmin's life story, but also awaken what others have known, felt, and experienced.

I have not tried to analyze or provide a "review" of this work, as it is unnecessary and the meaning will be experienced differently by each reader. However, I am confident that it will be life-changing for some and a mirrored reflection of truth for others. I am grateful to be part of this brave woman's journey and to share in her art.

Pat Pernicano, PsyD
author and trauma-focused therapist

Author Acknowledgements

There are many to thank, first and foremost my Lord and Savior for bestowing on me the talent to express myself and to be a storyteller. My wonderful, powerful artist collaborator and fellow combat veteran, Christina Helferich-Polosky, is the real deal. We bring out the best in each other; never underestimate the power of the sisterhood. I look forward to future collaborations. Con mucho respeto amiga.

I am grateful to Dr. Pat Pernicano, who graciously provided the Afterword, and to all my early reviewers: Dr Norma E. Cantú, Dr Sandra Morissette, AnnMarie Halterman (USAF veteran), and Captain Moira McGuire (USPHS ret.). They are all rock stars in their fields, and I am honored to have them associated with *Latina Warrior*.

I am forever grateful to friends and family who provided feedback on countless reading of poems, in particular mi prima Tish Tamez, the grunt Sue Caldwell, my mentees Ruby Gonzalez and Valentina Leanos, my college roomie Chris Guevara, vecinas Donna Hopkins and Phyllis Papa, Army veteran Rick Crosson, Marine veteran Mike Logan, and fellow Blue Ear Books author Jeb Wyman.

Rosario Carrington and Pamela Booth, along with Valentina Leanos, Rosy Zertuche, Raitza Garcia, Ruby Gonzalez and Xavier Guevera provided input for the Spanish version of my poem "Latina Warrior." So many words could have been used, and I wanted to ensure that what I ended up selecting matched what was in mi corazon y alma.

Special thanks to Valentina Leanos, owner of VITAL WIZARD, for your tireless, proficient, professional IT support, and for calmly talking me off the ledge every time I suffered a major tech crisis. Gracias amiga.

Mi primo Rick Tamez: super grateful for all the pictures you provided so we could capture the essence of "Valley Girl" in the corresponding art. How quickly you responded to my request speaks to the connective power of familia. Mil gracias primo.

My VA EMDR therapist: thanks for being there, listening, and providing the guidance I needed to navigate my healing journey. "The Breakup" was for you. Am grateful beyond words for what you do every day to help veterans.

Special thanks to Uniting US for providing events that educate the public and also bring veteran artists together from across the country to bond as a community. It was at one of these events that I met Christina.

Military Women's Memorial: thanks for providing spaces and programming to allow veterans to express ourselves and for the never-ending work you do on behalf of the veteran sisterhood.

My fellow veterans: You lessen my pain each time we hang. So many shared experiences and honest, authentic conversations. In our community, we are not alone.

Texas A&M University-Kingsville (TAMUK), my alma mater: am super appreciative of your unwavering support for my work. Who knew that my journalism degree all those years ago would act as a seed and grow into the writings throughout my life and in the two books I have now published. Thanks for the outstanding education! And now, am deeply grateful for you hosting the first book release event for *Latina Warrior*. Special thanks to Ruby Gonzalez, my social activities chair and biggest cheerleader, your tireless efforts to help me share my work are greatly appreciated. "Javelinas" captures how I feel about my alma mater. You all rock, and I am honored to be able to give back with my leadership and scholarship for military-affiliated students.

The University of Texas at San Antonio: thanks to the office of Veteran and Military Affairs, the Honors College, and the UTSA Top Scholar program. Although TAMUK is my alma mater, as founder of both VMA and Top Scholar, I have deep roots at UTSA and am pleased to be able to give back and share my leadership, gifts, and art with you to help students.

My author photo on the back cover: thanks to Jordan Spivey of Guera's Silver Co., for allowing me to "borrow" some great jewelry pieces for the photo shoot and thanks to fellow USAF veteran Matt Roberts for taking a great photo.

Muchisimas gracias a mi pastora Lupina Villalpando Stewart for her many blessings placed upon me and my work and for the photos she provided to be used in the art piece to go along with the poem "Mi Pastora."

My siblings, Lance, Ana, and Charles: you all are the best. Really appreciate you all once again being okay with me sharing with the world some of our family history. Lance, I hope I didn't embarrass you too much with "Big Bro." My heartfelt thanks for all the wonderful pictures you all provided, especially the one about our mother, "Tomasita." Am super grateful to all of you for not judging me when I finally spoke up about MST and PTSD. Con mucho amor.

To Mom and Dad: I miss you every day and am grateful for the great start in life you provided, but most of all for loving me unconditionally and for instilling in me the warrior spirit. You both led the family by example, and the power of that cannot be overstated.

Blue Ear Books: Hard to express my gratitude to Ethan Casey. I will never forget when we were starting work together on my first book, *Stories from the Front: Pain, Betrayal, and Resilience on the MST Battlefield*. I asked if you would ever publish a book of poems, and you did not hesitate in stating emphatically no. Never say never, my friend. Ha, this Latina had the last laugh as we did it! You are a great human and an outstanding editor and publisher. I am forever grateful to you and to interior designer Jennifer Haywood, as this book was complex with poems, prose, and art. Jenny, you did a great job, and I am so thankful. Sean Robertson: thanks for taking the fabulous art piece created by Christina and bringing my vision for the cover to life. Your insights were spot on and deeply appreciated. What an impressive team at BEB. I am so proud of our community of authors and our Veteran Book Initiative. Much love.

Finally, to my beloved son: I count my blessings every day for our relationship. I finally learned what was important in life, and you helped me do that. Thanks for allowing me to share a public version of "The Boy, the Man, and the Father." It's from the heart and sums up just how special you are to me. Te amo tanto mijito.

* * *

Earlier versions of several poems in this collection were published previously: "Into the Light" and "MST Warrior" in *Stories from the Front: Pain, Betrayal, and Resilience on the MST Battlefield*, Blue Ear Books (April 2022); "Invisible Veteran" in *Hispanic Executive* magazine; "The Sisterhood" in *Women Veterans Texas* magazine; "The Abyss" in the Blue Ear Books Substack newsletter and the National Association on Mental Illness Kansas newsletter.

Poems were displayed or read at exhibits at the Department of Veterans Affairs, Military Women's Memorial, Library of Congress, Kavanagh Gallery at the Fine Line Creative Arts Center, Bihl Haus Arts, Centro Cultural Aztlan, Uniting US Veteran Art at Dulles Airport, Operation Home Front Vets Nite Open Mic, South Texas Veterans Health Care System Mental Health & Wellness Summit, Veterans Counseling Veterans Military Sexual Trauma Conference, Puget Sound Veterans Health Care System Chief of Medicine Conference, Texas Association of Collegiate Veteran Program Officials Conference, Lamar University, Our Lady of the Lake University, Texas A&M-San Antonio, Texas A&M-Kingsville, Delaware Valley Veterans Coalition, American GI Forum, LULAC, Art Spark Texas, Jacqueline

Smith Foundation, American Legion, Texas Veteran Commission, and The University of Texas at San Antonio.

"Into the Light," "MST Warrior," "Save the Civilians," and "Invisible Veteran" have been posted online at www.lisacarringtonfirmin.com, and "Into the Light" was shared via *Latina Style* magazine.

Artist Acknowledgements

Gloria Steinem once said, "The art of life is not controlling what happens to us, but using what happens to us." This book is a concrete representation of that idea for me.

Lisa, my Uniting US sister, I am so unbelievably humbled that you entrusted me with the honor and responsibility of illustrating your poetry. You have no idea how much I appreciate not only your talent, but also your contributions to our military. Not just to the Air Force, or the Army, because you led us too; and not just to the female members, or a segmented population here or there—the contribution you made as leader, period. No further adjectives needed. I'll right-seat-ride any adventure with you any time.

Mom, my first role model—the quiet Vietnam Era veteran, without whose shoulders to stand upon, we'd have been a generation unable to grasp our own true heights. Dad, my original artisan mentor, the maker of molds and frames, a truer craftsman I've not yet met.

To all my brilliant children: Jacob, Michael, Tyler, Anthony, and Hannah Liberty (Willow)—you were perfect the minute you were conceived. Thank you for all the love and support you have always given me and my art career, and for being my best and most honest critics. I am so proud of you all for the humans you are growing into.

To my big brother Matt, sister Annie, all 'the cousins,' and all our extended family—Grandmother Dye, Aunt Tunkey, *all* the Cleveland clan, Peggy and Mike, Jill, Pat, Jack, Ben and Maggie, Christy and Gregg—thank you for being my most steadfast and ardent supporters.

To my Warrior PATHH guides and especially my 3/5—Paula, Lisa, Liz and Amy; thank you for helping me struggle well each day. I was only *truly* able to finish this project because of what we learned on the PATHH and knowing that the Travis Mills Foundation and you all will forever have my six. Post Traumatic Growth works—we are living proof of it. If you are a male or female Global War on Terrorism (GWOT) combat veteran, active-duty military, member of other governmental agencies that support(ed) the GWOT, or a first responder who has been involved in a critical incident, Warrior PATHH could help you too. No clinical diagnosis or prior mental health care is required to attend. https://travismillsfoundation.org/pathh

To AnnMarie and Tiffany, the UnitingUS.org co-founders: your organization literally saved my life, by getting me back in my studio at a time when I had all but given up on myself and my art. Thank you for being there for me when I really needed it—with open hearts, understanding ears, and as always, faithful friends.

To my Carlisle, PA cohorts and supporters: thank you so much for welcoming me and Hannah Liberty into your community with open arms. You embraced our art from the very beginning and that was so unexpected and refreshing. To Leslie at the gorgeous Boutique on Pomfret: you took a chance on me and my art, barely taking any commission, and you were the first person that made me feel like a real professional (and marketable) artist. To Natalie at the marvelous nDesign Art Haus Gallery at https://ndesignarthaus.com/: thank you for all the artistic camaraderie and inspiring fellowship. Most of all, thank you for standing in the gap for veteran artists—you have never made us outsiders feel anything short of professional and that's the real gift. Finally, to Kenya, my VA caregiver: You are truly the one that makes this art happen on the daily. You know, you see—thanks can't be given enough for what you do.

Thank you to my all my BFA professors from my circuitous journey around this country from my time as a military spouse: Marymount University in Arlington, Virginia; the University of Alabama in Huntsville; Austin Peay State University in Clarksville, Tennessee. If I could have stayed in one place long enough, I would have three degrees by now, lol—but I have always said my voyage was for a reason and I got to experience the best of three worlds and teaching institutions. Special thanks to my UAH Art History professor Dr. Stewart, who showed me that my old love of history could be combined with my new love of art; to Roxie Veasey, who first introduced me to something called 'mixed media' and told me I was getting the hang of it; to Jill Johnson, who taught me to paint from my heart; to my first sculpture instructor Chris Taylor, who didn't underestimate my aptitude in the shop; and to Desmond Lewis, who introduced me to the art of clay and steel. Most of all, I wish to thank the person I consider my collage mentor, Billy Renkl (http://www.billyrenkl.com/), the first professor to tell me that I might want to consider being a collage artist. The collages in this book are dedicated to you.

To my Army family, too many to name, all the amazing soldiers I served under, alongside, and with, thank you. You are never far from my mind. One is never really celebrated when one is medically retired—there is no party, no ceremony, many times no awards or decorations. I spent a lot of time feeling sorry for myself and closing myself off from that old life because it was too painful to look back. It wasn't you; it was me. I could have kept in touch, should have, especially with the outstanding soldiers and civilians of the 508th Transportation Truck Company out of Fort Eustis, Virginia.

And finally, to anyone I may have missed, especially those I served with during my time in the Army—there just aren't enough pages in this book or gratitude in my heart to do justice to how thankful I am to everyone.

About the Author

Colonel Lisa "La Coronela" Carrington Firmin retired from the USAF as its most senior Latina officer. She is a speaker, writer, poet, advocate, and Bronze Star-decorated combat veteran, founder of Carrington Firmin LLC, and a storyteller who writes, speaks, and provides consulting services in Leadership, Veterans, Transitions, Military Sexual Trauma (MST), and Diversity/Inclusion. Her poetry provides intimate reflection into the invisible wounds of MST, PTSD, trauma, hardship, and combat. She is the author of *Stories from the Front: Pain, Betrayal, and Resilience on the MST Battlefield* (Blue Ear Books, 2022) and founder of The University of Texas at San Antonio's Office of Veteran and Military Affairs and the UTSA Top Scholar program.

La Coronela serves as a member of the inaugural Department of Defense Advisory Committee on Diversity and Inclusion, the Department of Veterans Affairs Advisory Committee on Minority Veterans, and the Texas A&M University-Kingsville Foundation Board of Trustees. She is the first woman board member of the Hispanic Veterans Leadership Alliance, a member of the Military Officers Association of America and the Military Writing Society of America, and a life member of the Honor Society of Phi Kappa Phi, Veterans of Foreign Wars, and Women Veterans Alliance. She holds the National Diversity Council's Certified Diversity Professional designation and is a Certified True Colors® Facilitator.

Carrington Firmin has received many honors and accolades, including the Legion of Merit with oak leaf cluster, National Latina Symposium 2023 Veteran of the Year, 2023 award-winning author from the Military Writers Society of America, UTSA's President's Distinguished Diversity Award, the United States Hispanic Chamber of Commerce National Latina Leader award, the Governor of Texas' Yellow Rose award, the National Diversity Council's Trailblazer and Most Powerful and Influential Women in Texas awards, the Texas Diversity Council's Greater San Antonio LGBT Ally Award, the Hispanic Women's Network of Texas Trailblazer Award, the Distinguished Alumni Award from Texas A&M University-Kingsville, and the Community Service Award from the National Society of the Daughters of the American Revolution.

https://www.lisacarringtonfirmin.com/

About the Artist

Major Christina Helferich-Polosky was 100% disabled and medically retired by the United States Army in 2009 because of multiple physical and mental injuries and illnesses suffered during more than eleven years of successful active-duty service as a Transportation and Information Operations Officer. Most of her disabilities were later attributed to unknown chemical, environmental, and burn pit exposures that occurred during combat deployments to Kuwait/Iraq (OIF) in 2003 with the 7th Transportation Group (Forward) out of Fort Eustis, Virginia, where she was awarded the Bronze Star, and Bagram, Afghanistan (OEF) in 2008 with CJTF-101 out of the 101st Airborne Division (Air Assault) from Fort Campbell, Kentucky.

As part of her healing process, she created the free online art gallery cooperative WoundedNotWorthless.com LLC for female military, veteran, and wounded warrior artists. She invites all female military-related artists to join the site for mentorship, guidance on how to write and develop their own artist statements, and a safe space to share works and brands within a galvanized network of support.

Wounded Not Worthless - Female Vet/Wounded Warrior Artists

Not Worthless

Veterans Book Initiative

Blue Ear Books has a strong interest in developing and publishing books by American military veterans. Our mission is to assist veterans in their journeys to becoming published authors. We want to provide a platform for honest accounts of personal experience that will bridge the gap in understanding and empathy between veterans and the civilian public.

Learn more at:

https://blueearbooks.com/veterans/

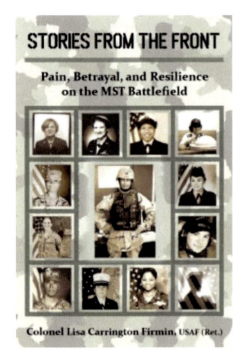

Coming soon from Blue Ear Books:

No One Leaves Unscathed: A Woman in the Marine Corps by Stesha Colby-Lynch

Troublemakers: The Greatest Dog and Pony Show in Iraq by Stephen Russell

Touching the Face of God: A Fighter Pilot's Story by Travis Vanderpool

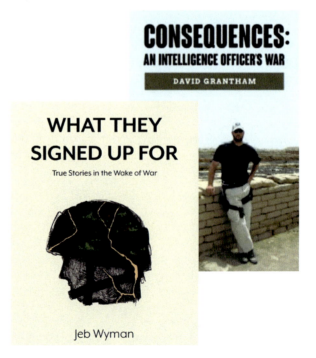

Stories from the Front by Bronze Star-decorated combat commander Colonel Lisa Carrington Firmin captures experiences across decades, from Vietnam to the present day, of sexual harassment, sexual assault, and race/ethnic, gender, and LGBTQ disparities in the U.S. military, and recounts 14 personal narratives of trauma, resilience, and empowerment.

Made in the USA
Monee, IL
17 October 2023

44730195R10119